THE MAN WHO MADE PARIS

PARIS

Haussmann at the height of his glory.

THE MAN WHO MADE PARIS

PARIS

THE ILLUSTRATED BIOGRAPHY OF GEORGES-EUGENE HAUSSMANN

WILLET WEEKS

Photographer of
scenes of Paris today

JEAN-CLAUDE MARTIN

LONDON
HOUSE

First published in Great Britain in 1999 by
LONDON HOUSE
114 New Cavendish Street
London W1M 7FD

A catalogue record for this book is available
from the British Library

ISBN 1-902809-33-3

Edited and designed by DAG Publications Ltd, London.
Printed and bound by Redwood Books,
Trowbridge, Wiltshire.

Jacket illustrations reproduced courtesy of the following:
Cabinet Immobillier Ravier, Paris: Aerial view of Paris.
Phototheque des Musées de la Ville de Paris: Place de la Rébublique.
CNMHS/S: Arc de Triomphe.

Illustrations reproduced courtesy of the following:
BHVP (Bibliothèque Historique la Ville de Paris): pages 50, 109, 111
and 112.
Bibliothèque Nationale de France: 45, 90, 128, 133 and 143.
Marville/BHVP: pages 20, 28, 31, 84, 114, 115, and 120.
Photothèque des Musées de la Ville de Paris: pages 2, 14, 17, 23, 24,
36, 52, 81, 82, 87, 88, 93, 94, 95, 100, 102, 103, 107, 108, 127 and
130.
Roger-Violet: pages 24, 38, 43, 64, 69, 83 and 85.

CONTENTS

Baron, Senator, Officer of Légion d'honneur and elected to Académie des Beaux-Arts—'Haussmannian' architecture abounds—royalty flock to renowned Hôtel de Ville receptions—rising opposition—widespread jealousy

Part 1
1347. Destruction of Knights Templars by Philippe IV—Louis XVI and his family imprisoned in Temple before execution in 1792

Part 2
1857. Napoleon III orders destruction of entire Temple enclave—Haussmann continues renovation of the city with parks and green spaces, covered market, flowing water—consistency of style harmonises all parts of Paris

Part 1
1869. Haussmann's financial methods and private life under attack—Napoleon III's position weakening—to ensure financing for completion of project, makes deal with enemies, disavowing Haussmann

Part 2
1870. Sacked, Haussmann makes memorable exit

Retirement—Franco–Prussian War—Communards destroy Haussmann's Hôtel de Ville by fire—his planning adhered to—a hundred years after death, a statue erected

PREFACE

In the course of more than twenty years as a career consultant in the USA and Europe, I've spent thousands of hours helping international managers come to terms, on the one hand with their aspirations, and, on the other, with their real abilities. How did they choose their careers? How closely do these choices today correspond to their inner needs? What changes might bring them more satisfaction?

I suppose it was inevitable that the career of Georges-Eugène Haussmann would catch my attention. Rarely do I encounter a person whose adult life work turns out to be, as did his, such a seamless projection of very early influences – and never on such a dramatic scale.

The word 'integrity' in both its meanings sums up Haussmann. It certainly applies to his innate honesty. At the same time he possessed integrity in the sense of consistency; everything hangs together. Whatever Haussmann's faults – and they were anything but hidden – fickleness and wavering were clearly not among them.

Haussmann's strengths, weaknesses and foibles blossomed early, stayed with him, and became more pronounced as his career evolved. That's why the direct links between his past and his actions once he was in power are, as we'll see, so evident.

Let me be more specific.

The clearest and earliest childhood imprint on Haussmann's professional life was the trouble he experienced breathing the polluted air of early 19th-century Paris. (Today his problem would probably be diagnosed as asthma. The great fear of the day, however, was the 'consumption' that littered opera-house stages with dying sopranos.) Periodic visits to the countryside seemed to be the solution for Georges-Eugène. But on each return to the city, the boy was again racked by fits of coughing. It's not at all surprising that later he would declare war on polluted air.

Here cause and effect are so apparent that the opening pages of Chapter 1, 'AIR', deal with his horror – up to, and throughout, his university years – of the polluted city air. Then he escapes to start his professional career, recovering his health in the more salubrious atmosphere of two provincial towns. At this point Part 2 of Chapter 1 leaps ahead to the adult Haussmann's return to Paris as prefect in 1853 and his eagerness to create two 'lungs' – the Bois de Boulogne and the Parc de Vincennes – to help the city breathe. At the same time, he reveals his passion for immensely wide avenues to channel fresh air into the heart of an overcrowded, suffocating city.

Chapter 2, 'MOBILITY', deals with Haussmann's lifetime hatred of any sort of blockage to progress – whether due to poor roads, snarled traffic or the many frustrations he faced in getting on with his job. Always in a hurry as a youth – to learn, to 'progress', to get from point to point – Haussmann's later passion for facilitating transport seems pre-ordained. Haussmann avoided the word 'traffic'; to speed 'circulation' was his goal. As in Chapter 1 and succeeding chapters, I call upon the impress of his formative years to illuminate his later actions. Without them, Parisians would today find it a challenge to go from one *'quartier'* to another except on foot. Today's dense automotive traffic would not be able to move at all!

Succeeding chapters follow the same pattern, opening with a particular early influence, then showing how it manifests itself in his transformation of Paris. You will find in the end that you are in possession of a rounded profile of a remarkable man and, at the same time, an account of the miraculous rebirth of Paris which he seemed destined to bring about despite awesome difficulties.

For many readers, an explanation of the title prefect (*préfet* in French) may be useful. The prefectorial system was an invention of the Romans, created to exercise central control over a far-flung empire. In France, each of the nation's 95 regional departments has its *'préfecture'*, run by a prefect who in turn controls a number of sub-prefectures with authority over smaller regions, comparable to counties in the USA.

The prefects and the sub-prefects wield police powers, but their importance extends far beyond keeping order since they are the representatives of the central government as it muscles in on all aspects of local administration. While the power of the prefects has been reduced in recent years, the apparatus itself still exists as in Haussmann's day.

Napoleon III bestowed on Haussmann the title préfect of the Seine. Since the *Département* of the Seine is identical with the territory occupied by the city of Paris, power conflicts between the préfect of the Seine and Paris's préfect of police were inevitable. However, Napoleon I, who created the system, wanted it that way – to prevent the préfect of the Seine from acquiring too much power. With the unfailing support of the Emperor, abetted by his own pugnacity, Haussmann emerged the victor from nearly all such struggles. In 1859, Napoleon III finally transferred all major city administrative functions to Haussmann's jurisdiction, but the préfect of the Seine never succeeded in acquiring the less ambiguous title, 'Minister of Paris', which he dearly wanted.

As I started work on this book, I asked dozens of Parisians what came to their mind at the mention of the name Haussmann. The answers were so bewilderingly varied that they brought to mind an old fable of three blind men and their encounter with an elephant. Grabbing the elephant's trunk, the first man was convinced that he had taken hold of a fearsome snake. One of his companions bumped up against the side of the beast. His verdict: his way was barred, he was certain, by an immense wall. Wrapping his arms around a leg, the third man knew that his companions were badly mistaken. No doubt entered his mind that he was embracing the trunk of a tree.

The missing element in their conclusions was the truth.

A taxi driver knew for sure that Haussmann created straight, wide avenues to make it easier for the police to shoot down rioters. Even more emotional were the reactions of certain, mostly professional and creative, people who voiced their fury at the prefect's destruction of so much of the old Paris. An astonishing number of respondents simply shrugged, saying, 'Haussmann must have been the man the long boulevard through the 8th *Arrondissement* is named after'. Then came the people who simply shrugged.

And so it went. A piece of truth here, a fragment there, but not once a response to evoke the mosaic of Haussmann's accomplishment.

For example, what may well be the most spectacular single contribution – went unmentioned by all: his creation of the greatest and most complex water-supply and sewage system the world had ever seen. Perhaps unseen is more apt, for that accomplishment, which ended centuries of devestating cholera epidemics, remains hidden beneath the pavements.

From time to time the comments became quite heated. Even now – 110 years after his death, Haussmann often is, quite simply, disliked. He is seen to be an autocratic man, boastful and pushy, but worse, he was, openly and proudly, an unreconstructed Imperialist at the dawn of the third Republic.

The grain of truth that lies in each of these perceptions has blinded genera-tions to the true *grandeur* of Haussmann's work. His enemies, before and after his death, tend to be verbal people – journalists, novelists, political essayists – almost all viscerally opposed to his politics.

(By contrast, the visual artists – Caillebotte, Monet, Manet, Pissarro, probably less politically volatile, captured – untroubled by polemics – the elegance and dynamism of the new Paris.)

To people who may have been overly influenced by the articulate critics, there is only one possible response and it is unanswerable. 'What would Paris be like today if Haussmann had never lived?' But perhaps, after all, there is an answer. Paris very likely would be a third-rate capital, unhealthy, congested and spurned as a place to live or to visit.

I consider myself lucky to have come across Haussmann as an outsider – an expatriate American living in Paris. The more I read and the more I moved about the city, the more determined I became to produce a rounded picture of this remarkable man; to do justice to his extraordinary achievement while not blinking away his faults – particularly his blindness to the sweep of history toward democracy.

At the time of Haussmann's death, the conservative newspaper, *Le Figaro*, got it right:

'The former prefect who created our boulevards, our streets, our open spaces – he who had in his hands a staggering budget that made possible all of these wonders – died a poor man. Without the modest dowry of his wife, he would have been reduced to begging for the most humble of jobs. But his name, so justly attached to one of our main boulevards, will remain indelibly linked to all of Paris, which was his work, his glory and his life.'

INTRODUCTION

Mouldering. The word describes the Paris of 1853, the year that the Emperor Napoleon III summoned Georges-Eugène Haussmann – later the Baron Haussmann – to improve matters. The population of the city was exploding. Many Parisians lived in shacks and shanties for want of decent accommodations. Speculators saw no reason to maintain or even repair sagging dwellings because of the demand for space at any price. Citizens who dared to walk after dark by the flickering light of oil-lamps took their lives in their hands. Roving bands of thieves awaited them in streets so narrow that two carriages could not pass, while the fetid air was alive with pollution. From above, pedestrians heard the cry 'Look out, water!' as householders flung their slops out of windows. Few streets had pavements. Even long-time residents could get lost threading their way home through a maze of alleys and dead-end streets. Strangers were obliged to seek directions from neighbourhood shop-keepers.

Haussmann's instructions were to transform a medieval heap of a city into a glorious capital worthy to be the seat of power of the Emperor Napoleon III. Most men would have quailed. But Haussmann was no ordinary man; he relished the prospect. In the following seventeen years he revolutionised the way the city looked and functioned. Gone were the decay and dilapidation. Yet he preserved, and even glorified, the magnificent monuments from the past by making them focal points for a network of noble avenues and boulevards.

A miracle? No, rather the result of an extraordinary drive, an uncanny ability to choose men and a rare administrative flair – all backed by the then-omnipotent Napoleon III.

Yet there is more – far more – to this original man than that: host to the rulers of Europe, leader of the quadrille far into the night, wine expert, charmer when it was useful – and yet possessor of the kind of courage that can face down – alone and unarmed – a mob of protesters.

And what a show the Baron knew how to mount, whether it was staging fireworks and dancing for some anniversary of the first Napoleon or creating an eye-filling spectacle, worthy of D. W. Griffith, to speed the nephew of the great Napoleon on his own way to glory.

While the results of Haussmann's boundless energy are everywhere to be seen, the man himself remains as elusive as his work is visible. Not that he was self-effacing. In terms of physical stature he stood out in any crowd. Handsome, he was a huge man for his time – almost six feet tall and well-muscled without a hint of fat.

But beyond the fact of his appearance, he slips away into a maze of contra-dictions. This is one reason for the fascination of his story. Boastful – sometimes embarrassingly so – he none the less could almost always win others over to his point of view. Although he was often seen to be haughty, there were, among the 14,000 labourers who wielded pickaxes and trowels in dirt, noise, heat and cold, many who wept when their boss was fired. While he drove his handful of close collaborators mercilessly, he succeeded in winning a respect that overcame their frequent disagreements.

The results of Haussmann's work not only still exist, but are today being imitated throughout Paris and its suburbs. Yet the man who could claim to be the greatest urban environmentalist of his century – and perhaps of all time – was trashed into a century of oblivion by his enemies. His story is one of triumph and Greek tragedy in its inevitability.

Not until nearly one hundred years after his death, did the city of Paris finally see fit to put politics aside in favour of a gesture of gratitude. Today at a bend in the boulevard bearing his name stands a statue of its builder erected in 1991. At the base, an inscription reveals nothing more than name, title and dates. One added line could have said it all:

GEORGES-EUGENE HAUSSMANN
THE MAN WHO MADE PARIS PARIS

1
AIR

Seen from a balloon in 1853, Paris might have seemed a slag-heap punctuated by a few handsome spaces handed down by royalty: Place de la Concorde ... Place Henri IV ... the gardens of the Palais Royal, the Luxembourg and the Tuileries. The rest consisted mostly of the jumbled roofs of medieval buildings. Here and there a noble structure gleamed: the Cathedral of Notre-Dame, the Louvre Palace, the immense Arc de Triomphe, raised in honour of the great Napoleon, uncle of the man who was to become Georges-Eugène Haussmann's boss.

Even at low altitude, the streets would have been hard to trace beneath the overhanging top storeys that sometimes almost touched one another. No matter, more often than not they went nowhere in particular. Even getting from one to another of the famous monuments could pose a problem. It is said that people became confused when only a few yards from home. Since the streets were liable to be slippery with filth, as well as crime-ridden, losing one's way could be particularly unnerving. But strong arms were available to carry pedestrians – for a few sous – across the most flooded intersections. The absence of sunlight and air and drainage trapped the smells of cooking, garbage and human waste while the festering humidity crept into the dubious entrances of decaying houses.

At the same time the railway was discharging hundreds of passengers daily into terminals that were already overcrowded. A new arrival had to make his way to his destination through meandering streets, many of which were too narrow to permit the passage of two carriages abreast. It was time-consuming and could be hazardous; pedestrians were a tempting target for the thieves who thrived in pockets of gloom and poverty.

Such was the state of Paris when Georges-Eugène Haussmann was sworn in as prefect of the Seine on 28 June 1853.

Forty-four years earlier, when the future baron came into the world, the

Below: The entrance to the building at 177 Boulevard Haussmann that now stands on the site of Haussmann's boyhood home. He was stigmatised as soulless for ordering its destruction. Calmer minds later asked what if, while demolishing the homes of so many others, he had ordered his own to be spared?

Left: Haussmann around 1853, at the commencement of his tenure as prefect of the Seine.

city was not too different from that which existed when he took office. To be sure, fewer people lived there at that time and the shanties that soon began to mushroom like leprous growths around the Louvre were not yet so numerous. The great Napoleon, who reigned at the time of Georges-Eugène's birth, had cherished plans to modernise the city. He dreamed of a grandiose capital, but he was too often otherwise occupied – mostly on the battlefield. In the end he could take credit for some sixty new streets and a project, completed only after his departure, for the elegantly arcaded Rue de Rivoli. He also introduced the idea of numbering each building so that residents at last came to have an address. The construction actually achieved under Napoleon, however, was a patchwork, lacking any coherence. Even his plans, such as they were, could in no way be considered a template for the overall transformation of Paris.

Today it is generally agreed that the first five years of one's life indelibly mark the adult to be. In Haussmann's case, those years were the last of the Napoleonic era. The French had come close to overturning the monarchies of Europe, as their revolutionaries had succeeded in doing at home. The parades of colourful troops and the swelling of national pride combined to fill the boy's mind with visions of imperialistic glory.

In Volume one of his three Volumes of *Memoirs*, Haussmann describes one of his earliest recollections. He was waiting with his grandfather in the gardens of the Trianon Palace for a reception to begin. The grandfather was not just another guest; he was General Dentzel, a baron of the French Empire. Only four, Georges-Eugène was big for his age and the general was proud of the strapping youngster. He had even arranged to dress his grandson in the uniform of his regiment. Every detail of the tiny outfit was perfect, from the tall military hat with its small visor to the intricately looped fasteners that decorated his jacket.

Suddenly voices came from the hedge behind them. Two strollers emerged from a path and turned into the main promenade. One of them was Napoleon Bonaparte, emperor of the greatest empire on earth. Little Georges-Eugène snapped to attention and delivered a crisp salute. '*Vive l'empereur!*,' he cried.

Napoleon paused, impressed. 'Well, my young friend, you have already enlisted in the army?'

To the pride of his grandfather, the boy had a ready answer. 'No, sir, I plan first to become a page to the Emperor.'

The lad would indeed enter into the service of a Napoleon, but not as a page. Eventually some would begin to call him 'vice-emperor'.

Both the Dentzel and Haussmann families were Protestant and both had produced remarkable men. The Haussmanns had fled Germany for France to escape the persecutions that followed the Reformation. They shared two traits with immigrants the world over – before and since: they were hard workers and they maintained strong family bonds. One of Georges-Eugène's forebears founded a textile mill that helped lay the groundwork for the prosperity of Alsace. Another, a chemist, had invented a bleach for fabrics, enabling him to live out his life on royalties.

As for Baron Dentzel, he had earned a reputation both as a courageous military man and a decent human being. After the defeat of the Prussians by Napoleon, he won the gratitude of the population of Weimar, and lovers of beauty everywhere, by sparing the magnificent library and palace, as well as other beautiful buildings in the city of Goethe. Later he became governor-general of Vienna, and there again he won that rare accolade: the appreciation of the people of a conquered city.

Not being hereditary, the title of Baron could not be passed on to his grandson. But the general did succeed in arranging to have his commander agree to act as godfather to little Georges-Eugène. This was no small matter, since the commander happened to be Prince Eugène de Beauharnais, the Empress Josephine's brother.

It is significant that the person who was to become Georges-Eugène's model, inspiration and companion was neither the colourful Baron Dentzel nor his own less-colourful newspaperman father. It was his father's father. This remarkable man had been a member of the Convention that tried to govern France during the Revolution. Although Nicolas Haussmann almost certainly did not cast his vote to send King Louis XVI to the guillotine, he later was punished by the restored monarchy. Having been among the revolutionaries was evidence enough of guilt. More real was the evidence of his energy. Before the age of 30, he had become the administrator of the *département* of Seine-et-Oise near Paris. His foresight, sense of organisation and ability to lead without shouting caught the attention of Napoleon Bonaparte who drafted him to assure the flow of supplies for two of his armies in the east of France. Above all, Nicolas was a highly skilled administrator. He must also have been a very loving grandparent; Georges-Eugène's admiration of him never waned, even after his death.

With both such grandfathers active Bonapartists – and therefore enemies of the aristocracy – little Georges-Eugène's salute to Napoleon signalled an enduring commitment to the imperial model; individual liberty within clearly established order would always win his enthusiastic support.

As an infant he had a health problem because the foul air of Paris affected his breathing. The Haussmann home was near the then western edge of the city, at the upper part of the Faubourg St-Honoré (until 1847, the Faubourg St-Philippe du Roule). Yet even there the air seems to have been impure. His parents' concern for the baby's health was exacerbated by some cases of tuberculosis in the family history. Their solution was to send the boy out of the city to live with the senior Haussmanns. At their home, between Paris and Versailles, he not only breathed pure air but was free to toddle about outdoors. Then, too, his adored grandfather took him on outings which sometimes included witnessing the parading of the troops at Versailles. The effects of loving care and fresh air served as a tonic and soon his red cheeks and staunch body fully justified grandfather Dentzel's pride.

Right: The Rue de la Colombe near the City Hall: a typical street of pre-Haussmannian Paris.

The reception at the Trianon turned out to be the first and last time Georges-Eugène was to see the Emperor. The boy was brought back to Paris, but not before he saw violence blossom on all sides as the invading Cossacks terrorised the country-

side. The troops pushed their way into the Haussmann home, raped the servant girl and forced the grandmother to open her house as a lodging. By then Napoleon had been sent off to the island of Saint Helena and soon Tsar Alexander I was holding religious services with his imperial guard in the courtyard of the Elysée Palace.

The return of the monarchy aroused 'no feeling of solidarity', as Haussmann himself later put it, in the hearts of the family. In fact, grandfather Haussmann and his wife were briefly exiled to Switzerland – a wrenching period for Georges-Eugène. Grandfather Dentzel had returned from the wars with a shattered arm and Georges-Eugène's father had only the dole with which to support his wife and two children. The house in the country having become a luxury, they regrouped in the home of Georges-Eugène's parents.

At the age of nine, the boy was lagging in his studies. Once again his health had become fragile. Alarmed, his parents sent him off to a private school not far from Paris. The school was a lively establishment run by a M. Legal, a devoted anti-pedagogue. He was a 20th-century educator who believed that learning could best be achieved by observation and direct experience. Under this dynamic man the entire universe came to life for Georges-Eugène. Physics, astronomy, literature – even Latin – were made exciting in a way incomprehensible to the dusty academics of the day. Curiosity and a determination to learn soon became a part of the young Haussmann's nature.

Another aspect of the school was its cleanliness. M. Legal was as strict in this matter as he was lenient in adhering to time-worn academic disciplines. Two years of absolutely immaculate surroundings and untainted air had not only restored the boy's health, but had opened his eyes and mind to the enchantment and revelations of the countryside against which the sloth and squalor of Paris compared very unfavourably.

Left: The sub-prefecture of Blaye, near Bordeaux, is pleasantly situated with a view of a garden, partially shown above, but it was also the scene of a supreme test of Haussmann's political instincts. In 1848 France passed from a Monarchy to a Republic. The sub-prefect managed that change, plus the ensuing transition to Empire without loss of honour. He was thus able to go on to become prefect of Bordeaux and, ultimately of the Seine (in actuality, of Paris).

Georges-Eugène's recovery permitted him to enter a leading Paris academy, the Lycée Henri IV, for his high school education. Enrolled as a boarder because the air was clearer than at home, he had little cause to move about the city. That would come in his university years. He was a good student, soon finding himself seated, on the bench reserved for honours students, alongside the young Duc de Chartres, son of the man who a few years later would ascend to the throne of France. Despite their difference in social status, they became *copains* (pals). This schoolboy friendship would become a key to Georges-Eugène's success in networking his way up the fiercely competitive civil service system.

Alfred de Musset, another classmate, could not have been more different. His long hair and affected manners earned him the nickname 'Missy'. Constantly harassed by his instructors, he gave them no choice but to promote him, not to the next class, but to the one above it. Alfred was already enraptured by the romantic movement in literature and art, of which he would become a leading exponent. The volumes of poetry that flowed from him were to be enriched by a tragic affair with George Sand, the cross-dressing leader of the creative set. No trend could have been further removed from the nature of young Haussmann than the romantic. Yet de Musset may well have had an influence on his classmate; later Haussmann himself would write poetry of sorts, but that would come long after de Musset had been buried under his willow tree at Père Lachaise cemetery, three metres from where his friend would later lie. The childhood *copains* were to remain neighbours in perpetuity.

Georges-Eugène was more drawn to music. He enjoyed playing the cello in the school orchestra. One day after a Sunday service at the Lycée, the chapel was empty except for Haussmann and a friend. The organist also had departed, or so the boys thought. On an impulse Georges-Eugène persuaded his companion to pump the bellows of the organ. For the first time Haussmann tried to play the instrument. Perhaps he himself was surprised to hear that he was producing perfect harmonies. In any case, one person was clearly impressed – the organist, who had not left the building after all. He was so struck that he offered to tutor the boy in harmonics. The lessons continued until Georges-Eugène's knowledge 'exceeded that of his professor'. This is how the baron later described the situation, with his ingrained preference for accuracy over modesty.

However, he was not finished with his pursuit of music. Among the thicket of subjects he would later study was musical composition at the Paris Conservatoire under the great master, Cherubini. The day was to come when certain Parisians would regret Georges-Eugène's decision not to pursue that career path. 'How splendid it would be if Haussmann was making music today instead of deafening us with the racket of his demolitions.'

His decision to go for a law degree seems to have been rather haphazardly plucked from among a multitude of interests. He sopped up knowledge with the ease and lack of discrimination of a blotter. His problem: he found everything absorbing and would continue to do so throughout his life. He could be seen at Cherubini's music class, attending lectures in anatomy at the College of Medicine or even studying hydrology at the Ecole des Mines, a leading engineering school.

Naturally such a dispersion of his time caused him to miss an occasional lecture in law. No problem; he soon caught up with the others.

A subject for which no academic credit is given was one that impressed and depressed him profoundly. This was Paris itself. The Sorbonne was and is situated on the left bank of the Seine, while his home was on the then distant horizon of the right bank. In winter the Seine was sometimes frozen over, offering him a short-cut between the two. Swathed in protective wool by his mother, no matter how mild or how chilly the day, he would thread his way though the colourful streets of the Latin Quarter. He ate in the cheap restaurants (including the cheapest of all, one dubbed the 'Aquatique' because it served no wine) with his fellow-students, visited his scholarly barber, whose sign was in Greek, and occasionally took the 14-passenger omnibus that lumbered with difficulty along the serpentine streets. Colourful or not, all this quaintness was lost on Georges-Eugène. He was dismayed by the dirt, the disorder and, of course, that ancient enemy of his lungs – the germ-laden air. In winter, when the smoke from coal and wood fires shortened the hours of daylight, he felt no sentiment for a past that handicapped the life of the present.

And what an active life it was! Aside from his studies he maintained a social schedule that clearly marked him as a fashionable young Parisian. The theatre,

Above: The old City Hall as it appeared to Queen Victoria during her state visit in 1855. With his transformation of Paris only in its early stages, Haussmann had to route her carefully through the city in order not to expose to her view the unsightly devastation under way. This photograph by Marville was taken from what became the Avenue Victoria.

balls, shooting, duelling, swimming in summer, skating in winter – all these left some time in the evenings – except when a new opera opened – to learn the profession of his family's notary. Why the curiosity to learn about mortgages and contracts? Certainly not because he yearned to become a professional notary; as ever, he was driven by curiosity. Bedtime was midnight; wake-up at six. And there were no holidays from work, since for Georges-Eugène all was fun.

Nowhere in this exhaustive, and exhausting, list of activities is there any mention of politics. This is noteworthy because the other men of the family had their secret political clubs and underground press. While their opposition to the restored monarchy was unrelenting, conspiracy held no charm for the young Haussmann; he had seen the damage wrought in the lives of his grandfathers and his father by their loyalty to Napoleon. To be sure, in his heart Georges-Eugène also remained loyal to the former Emperor. But not in his actions.

Until 29 July 1830.

On 30 July 1830, Parisians by the thousands swarmed into the streets to rid themselves of the last Bourbon king. The uprisings lasted three days. For Georges-

Eugène those three days were pivotal. They brought him close to his father for the first time and, again for the first – though by no means the last – time he was able to show his mettle. Nicolas-Valentin Haussmann was by then editor of *Le Temps* – an opposition journal of course. King Charles X, bent on putting down violence with violence, sent a brigade of mounted police to break into the offices of the newspaper. Young Haussmann stood at the side of his father while a crowd on the sidewalk jeered and swore at the police. Daunted, the officers finally unleashed their anger by destroying the presses – a meaningless act since the staff had stashed away replacements in the basement.

By the third and last day of rioting, barricades everywhere were hobbling communications between the leaders of the insurrection and their key supporters around the city. Georges-Eugène volunteered to carry an editorial through the chaotic streets to the revolution's command centre in the City Hall. It was his first entry into a building that later would turn out to be his own seat of power. Then, on his return in the early hours of the morning, he found himself caught in the worst of the fighting, around the Church of St-Roche in the Rue St-Honoré (1st *Arrondissement*). Armed only with a pistol, he dodged the bullets flying from doorway to doorway. A gendarme charged at Georges-Eugène, knocking the gun from his hand. The two grappled. Somehow Haussmann managed to wrest the man's sword from him and escape. Seconds later a bullet grazed his left thigh. He limped back to the offices of *Le Temps* where his father tended the leg which was spurting blood. Every so often Nicolas-Valentin would gaze at the trophy his son had won.

Actually the wound was not serious. But there it was, and along with the captured sword, the young Haussmann had visible evidence of courage under fire. At the age of 21 he found himself decorated for bravery with the medal of 'The Three Glorious Days'. A talisman during the early days of the reign of Louis-Philippe, the decoration would come in handy in matters having to do with career advancement. No subject interested Haussmann more.

The elder son of the new 'citizen king' had been none other than Georges-Eugène's pal at the Lycée Henri IV. Thanks to his decoration, Haussmann found himself one day chosen to be a member of a military guard facing the duke at the investiture of his friend's father as head of state. The duke was delighted by their meeting – and Georges-Eugène even more so. In the end it was the newly named Duc d'Orléans who solved the young hero's career dilemma. Why shouldn't he join the public administration? Not only did the duke make the suggestion, but he went further and pulled strings to help Georges-Eugène win his first post. But Orléans was far from being the only string-puller. Reticence being totally foreign to Haussmann's nature, he recruited his father and every other family connection into a campaign of letter-writing aimed at the Minister of the Interior. Eventually he was granted an audience.

Nevertheless, the waiting time seemed painfully long before his appointment was actually signed. The ink was hardly dry when the new secretary of the prefecture of Poitiers leapt into a stage-coach and gladly left behind a polluted

Above: The receptions, dinners and balls at the City Hall given by the Haussmanns were renowned throughout Europe. This celebration was a particularly important occasion for them, the signing (left rear) of the marriage contract between their daughter Valentine and Camille Dollfus.

Paris, heading towards the pure air of a provincial town and a prodigious future.

To appreciate the significance of the jobs that succeeded one another throughout Haussmann's career, it's important to understand the role of the prefects in France. These officials represent the interests of the national government in each of the country's 95 *départements* (administrative counties). Under an authoritarian central government they held enormous power – maintaining order, assuring that governmental policies were carried out and – not openly – influencing elections.

Georges-Eugène's first post, as general secretary of the prefecture in Poitiers, consisted entirely of administering the routine functions of the office. He correctly complained that the work was not likely to make full use of his abilities. But then he routinely voiced that kind of protest on taking up each new assignment – that is, until at last he was chosen to become, in effect, mayor of the capital of France.

The prefecture of Poitiers was situated in a dismal old barracks near the edge of town. In principle, Georges-Eugène was supposed to room there, but he sought a livelier scene. He checked into a hotel and began to circulate among the bourgeoisie of Poitiers. Handsome, smartly dressed and, above all, Parisian, he cut quite a figure as a dandy. He was also a good listener, always interested in the other person. Soon he was sought out as a dinner guest in the best homes. He even showed himself to be a social organiser with special skills as a leader of the dance at balls.

In a review of his performance with his Paris boss, Casimir Perier, Minister of the Interior, he had received some words of advice which Georges-Eugène never

forgot: 'A young administrator must find agreeable, and even pretty when that is possible, the wives and daughters of officials.'

At work, Haussmann quickly had the routine of the prefecture humming. This was an important contribution to his boss, the prefect. In return Georges-Eugène discovered in himself something even more important – an ability to take charge of social events and to make people feel happy that they were among those present. His training had begun as future host to the greatest names in Europe.

Without warning, a decree from Paris landed on his desk. The function of prefectorial secretary was abolished throughout France. He was being assigned to the post of sub-prefect, meaning that he would be stationed in a county and would report to the prefect of the *département* of which the county was a part. He was ordered to go to a place called Yssingeaux. But where was that? How was it spelt? (His research produced three different ways.) Clearly this was far from being an august posting within the civil service. Clearly, too, it wasn't up to his abilities. But one overriding fact excited him: Georges-Eugène Haussmann was about to take charge of something! To him a position of command in the most remote town was preferable to pushing papers in a major capital.

The town of Le Puy, situated high in the mountainous region of south-eastern France, is famous for its vistas of volcanic terrain and dense forests. It is also the seat of the prefecture of the *département* of the Haute Loire. After reporting to his new boss, the prefect, Haussmann lost no time renting a one-man carriage. Powered by two horses, this vehicle was to whisk him upwards to Yssingeaux, only seventeen miles away. The rocky climb proved a challenge. At one point, after a difficult stretch, the animals required an hour's rest. He had started out early in the afternoon but arrived after nightfall. A street brawl welcomed him to his new fief. The sub-prefect's first duty turned out to be that of ambulance driver. On delivering the victim of the fight to the local hospital, he learned that such battles were a part of the daily agenda of his new compatriots.

From this start, the once-frail Parisian spent nearly all his time in the saddle. It was early summer and the mountain air itself was a tonic for which no doctor held a prescription. He went about his business from one end of the county to another, making certain that the drafting of young men for military service was fairly carried out, refereeing the distribution of wood from community-held forests, listening to the problems of artisans and farmers. In one remote corner of his territory he sought out a Protestant community. Arriving for Sunday church services, he was astonished to see stacked up in the vestibule rifles that had been carried to prayer by the congregation. The Protestants had reason to fear surprise attacks by armed troops. But his astonishment was mild compared to that of the townspeople at his arrival. To receive a visit from a Protestant official of the central government was an event without precedent.

Left: Superb horseman though he was, Napoleon III could not steady his steed enough to meet the needs of a photographer of his day. Here we see how the problem was solved.

Haussmann's success in bringing order to the region came largely from his non-partisan approach. He viewed his job as something totally divorced from politics. 'Always in my brief career', he wrote in his first directive to the mayors under his jurisdiction, 'I have held myself apart from all political activity, from its obligations as well as its temptations.' That kind of disciplined non-involvement would continue.

Thanks to his effectiveness, Georges-Eugène was spared the pain of coping with the rigours of a winter in the uplands. Someone in the ministry felt that his talents were needed in Nérac, a sub-prefecture not far from the Atlantic coast. His appointment set off a volley of messages between Le Puy and Paris. The residents of Yssingeaux were furious about the transfer of a young man who had so improved the climate of human relations in the county. Although their protests were in vain, Haussmann's reputation was not harmed by the tug-of-war for his services.

His superior, the prefect of Le Puy, neatly summed up the Haussmann of that time: 'A young man of considerable ambition who understands his strengths and who sees a bright future for himself.'

This was a rave notice compared to Georges-Eugène's estimate of the prefect himself, whom he judged incapable, 'knowing nothing about how to administer a department'.

In fact, once more Haussmann's new assignment disappointed him. He would again be a sub-prefect in an insignificant town. In today's business jargon, he was the object of a 'lateral promotion' – in every sense. To reach Nérac, where he was to spend the next eight years, he would have to cross France from east to west.

The thought dismayed him. He knew that a black cloud stood between him and his destination. It took the form of an ungainly stage-coach without springs, guaranteed to offer him days of physical and mental pain as it jig-sawed its illogical way over mountain and plain. Only time would reveal the nature of his ultimate destination.

PART 2

Paris 1853. Poor Jacques Hittorff. His work as chief architect of the city of Paris had already established his reputation. Perhaps his greatest work was the design of the monumental Palais de Justice. Now he had business to do at the City Hall where the new 44-year-old prefect of the Seine was burrowing through maps, blueprints and a maze of cost estimates. The meeting with prefect Haussmann was important; he was there to present his elevations for a new street to link the Arc de Triomphe with the Bois de Boulogne, and he was nervous. An outsider might shrug. After all, this was just one more street in a city that was launching into a frenzy of reconstruction. Both men knew, however, that a third person would be present in spirit, the Emperor Napoleon III.

The transformation into an elegant park of a scraggily wooded area on the west side of Paris was the first of the Emperor's great projects. As such, the results would be a key in his programme to make the city of Paris the glory and the envy of all Europe. It was, he declared, pointless to create a magnificent green space unless the people were given ready access to it by means of a suitable approach.

Right: The Passage du Dragon, near the eleventh-century church of St-Germain-du-Prés. As almost everywhere in pre-Haussmannian Paris, the drainage system consisted simply of a trench in the middle of the street. To warn passers-by, residents were required by law to shout 'Attention à l'eau!' ('Look out, water!') before flinging their slops out of the window.

The plan Hittorff unrolled for Haussmann called for a triumphal avenue on an imperial scale. Or so he thought. The street was to be named 'Avenue de l'Impératrice', in honour of the Empress Eugénie, the wife of Napoleon III. After all, Hittorff reasoned, his projected street would be 30 feet wider than any of the other avenues that were to radiate from the Arc de Triomphe. Within minutes his miscalculation became clear.

Haussmann was aghast. 'One hundred and twenty feet wide! My dear sir, we must have at least double that, even triple. Yes, triple it – let us have an avenue 360 feet wide.'

Hittorff was dumbfounded as the prefect went on:

'Those lawns that you propose between the houses and the street – make them four times as wide as your plan calls for. And add a carriage-way to serve the residences. That way we'll have 440 feet between the facing buildings – 320 feet more than you have in your project.'

As he talked, the prefect's good humour returned. He found the creation of space, and the channelling of air into the city, always to be a source of profound satisfaction.

Hittorff questioned the word 'your'. But subject to no doubt was Haussmann's superior understanding of the word 'glory' when used by Napoleon and his prefect. Only one problem stood between Haussmann's concept and its adoption. How could an avenue of such breadth open on to the Etoile without dwarfing most of the other streets that form the star? The solution they worked out is there to see today. The entrance to the Avenue Foch was reduced to the

Above: The quarries that became the Parc des Buttes Chaumont, one of the highest points in Paris. The stone was used for the reconstruction of Paris. Called 'pierre de taille', cut limestone, it is a feature of Haussmannian architecture. It has a luminous quality that makes Paris seem particularly brilliant in the sunlight (and sombre in the rain).

Above: The Parc des Buttes Chaumont today. The quarries shown in the preceding photograph were covered over with earth excavated from the reconstruction of Paris and hauled to the site to cover the raw stone and to permit landscaping.

width of the other streets leading off the Etoile before the full panorama of the great avenue meets the eye.

As was nearly always was the case with people of merit, Hittorff remained a valued collaborator of Haussmann's despite an unpromising start.

Haussmann's office looked out on a scene of desolation. Even before his appointment had begun an extension of the Rue de Rivoli had been projected, but not begun. Now the work was under way under his window, but progressing slowly. The reason for the delay threatened to block all the Emperor's dreams and to frustrate Haussmann's forward march. The problem was money. Haussmann's predecessor, the ex-Prefect Berger, was convinced that the cost of the project would bankrupt the city. His conservatism was one reason Napoleon III saw fit to replace him immediately, but his arguments carried weight in the Paris municipal council and Georges-Eugène had to find a way to counter them. He did so within eight days of taking the oath of office. After poring day and night over the projected city budget – and studying a liberal economic theory propounded by a group who called themselves the 'Saint-Simoniens' – he was ready to do battle. He first pointed out to the council that the budget contained a ten-million franc emergency reserve that could be used in case of need. But then came his main point – one which made not only the extension of the Rue de Rivoli possible, but also served to underwrite the entire transformation of Paris.

Today we would call the concept that gave him his victory Keynesian. M. Berger's error, as well as that of all his predecessors, was to base his forecast of tax revenues on current land values. Haussmann, on the other hand, argued that they should be calculated on the increased values resulting from the improvements the city would underwrite.

In the end, he won the council's approval. He called it his battle of Actium: Octavius had triumphed over Antony and Rome was in his grasp. Obviously the prefect had a weakness for classical allusions; they went well with the imperial scene now dominated by a French Emperor.

Along with the Bois de Boulogne, the Rivoli project was a source of great joy to Haussmann. Shanties, huts, decrepit houses had encroached on the palace of the Louvre to such an extent that the great building was shrouded in gloom and surrounded with filth. Balzac imagined the Louvre crying out for someone to remove the leprous façades from its gaze. Haussmann happily complied; he demolished all that was unworthy of the building, surveying every day the work from his office window. Later Georges-Eugène wrote: 'I saw all that disappear with great satisfaction.'

The need for wholesale destruction of buildings, on which the construction of a new, airier Paris depended, posed another problem second only to funding. Once again, he found the key. On the books since the time of Napoleon I was a law permitting the expropriation of property to make way for construction deemed 'in the public interest'. Oddly, the great Napoleon himself made little use of this provision – perhaps because it had not been his idea. Without it, the city would have had to pay out vast sums to entice occupants to leave their building. As to what constituted 'the public interest', Haussmann was the arbiter. He also determined the value of the property and thus the compensation to be paid.

He knew he had the support of Napoleon III in all his decisions. Without that, Haussmann's genius would have been strangled by bureaucratic red tape. In

Below: Haussmann and Napoleon III shared a liking for water – the Emperor because of his nostalgia for its presence in London parks, his prefect because of his passion for its purifying qualities. Below is the lake of the Bois de Vincennes, which is even larger than that of the Bois de Boulogne, its predecessor.

return the Emperor could always count on the loyalty of the most ardently Napoleonic collaborator of all – his prefect.

In charge of the landscaping of the Bois de Boulogne was Jean-Charles Alphand, a friend from Bordeaux. This great engineer first had to undo the work of his predecessor, much as Haussmann had to undo the budget of the man he succeeded. Napoleon III wanted expanses of water. Some say he was influenced by Hyde Park's Serpentine, an hypothesis that makes sense. After all, he had passed far more years as an exile in London than he had lived in France. Instead of shimmering water, the original engineer on the project presented him with a river: a trickle on high ground that swelled into a small torrent by the time it reached the limits of the park. Alphand's solution was to divert the downward course of the water into a series of charming lakes. He even created two spectacular man-made waterfalls. The larger, called the Grande Cascade, immediately became the source of much admiration.

Aside from his role as general-in-charge, Haussmann's specific contributions to the remodelling of the Bois were twofold. First he enlarged (nothing was grand enough for him) the park by extending it to the Seine. Secondly, he ordered a wall knocked down between the woods and the open area which today is occupied by the Longchamp race-track. This act was catnip to jokesters: 'Now the prefect even wants to aereate the Bois de Boulogne.' Haussmann's passion for fresh air had become a part of his identity.

In all, Haussmann and his collaborators created a staggering total of 26 green spaces, large and small. Every neighbourhood was to have ready access to a place, no matter how compact, of calm and beauty. Even larger than the Bois de Boulogne was a second vast park on the opposite side of Paris, the Parc de

Below: A grotto and cascade in the Bois de Boulogne, one of the many agreeable touches that the architect – and long-time friend of Haussmann – Alphand brought to the landscaping of the first of the two 'lungs' of Paris completed by the two men (the other the Bois de Vincennes on the opposite side of the city). This photograph was taken by the celebrated Charles Marville, official photographer of the transformation of Paris under Haussmann.

Vincennes. Haussmann saw the two parks as 'the lungs of Paris', an interesting metaphor in view of his early problem with breathing. Others dubbed them the 'rich man's' and the 'poor man's' parks. It was, and is, true that most wealthy people lived in the western part of the city. Yet there is little doubt that Parisians of all economic levels came to enjoy both open spaces – but only after all parts of the city could easily be reached by public transport. No one was more preoccupied by the problem of circulation of traffic, as well as of air, than Georges-Eugène Haussmann.

Putting aside class and category, the eastern portion of the city boasts (apart from the Bois de Vincennes) two of the most striking parks of Paris. The Buttes Chaumont is the most spectacular of all. The park was created by dumping thousands of tons of earth, excavated from construction sites, over the lofty outcroppings of old granite quarries that dominated the view to the north. For the loveliest green space of all, many would vote for the park of Montsouris far to the south.

No matter how beautiful, how spectacular, or how useful a project might be, Haussmann often had to deal with protests. One day, speaking before the senate, he observed: 'Everyone says the city undertakes too many projects, but then they complain that not enough is being done in their neighbourhood.'

His opponents were not in reality his foes, but rather those of the Emperor. The enemies of Louis-Napoleon lacked the courage to attack him directly; they preferred to snarl at the heels of his most prominent collaborator. Haussmann himself was partly responsible for being chosen as the chief quarry of the opposition. His abilities were so evident that he seemed to find it useless to try to hide, rather than proclaim, them. Proclaim them he did and, in the process, heightened his visibility as a target.

Created by Catherine de Médicis, the Luxembourg Gardens must rate high in public admiration among the parks of Paris. Mothers come to watch their children sail their boats in the little lake. Solitaries read their books in peace, while lovers stroll in the lightly wooded areas well away from the central mall.

At one time this tranquil corner of Paris exploded into a battleground. Haussmann needed a portion of the surface, mostly a tree nursery, to relieve traffic congestion. Overnight the thousands of acres of park he had created elsewhere in Paris were forgotten. The air was filled with the cries of protesters shouting 'Save the Luxembourg!'. As the movement grew, the printing presses started to turn. One pamphlet was entitled 'Apropos the Luxembourg'. Another, intended for Paris legislators, decried the 'Mutilation of the Luxembourg'. Well organised, the protest snowballed. Petitions and legal tracts multiplied. An unbelievable one hundred thousand people showed up to jeer the first shovelful of earth. In contrast, about 100 Haussmann supporters – 'speculators', according to the crowd – were there. They were confronted by charges that at least 15 million francs changed hands to grease the desecration of the park.

Finally Louis-Napoleon had to step in. When he visited the site, the cry went up, 'The Luxembourg is saved'. In fact, the Emperor 'proposed', and the senate ratified, only technical changes to Haussmann's plan. Behind the ruckus the hand of the prefect's opponents was not hard to detect. However, in the end the affair served only to reconfirm the solidarity between the Emperor and the man who was receiving the arrows intended for himself. The senate may not have been mollified, but Haussmann's authority emerged stronger than ever.

They made a good pair. Haussmann possessed the charisma and physique Louis-Napoleon might well have longed for. The Emperor, a sawn-off, somewhat comical figure with a pointed beard, held the immense power for which his prefect in his turn yearned.

The Luxembourg incident also illustrated the detailed interest that Napoleon III took in the transformation of the city. He and Haussmann met almost every day to discuss this or that innovation. No other official in the government had an imperial messenger always at his side. Thus the communication between the two men was immediate, direct and – most important – impervious to interception. The matter of security received high priority because the work of reconstruction was undertaken in phases; there was no 'master plan' except in the head of Haussmann. Expropriation papers were delivered to each proprietor so close to the beginning of work that speculation became almost impossible. Nevertheless leaks within the government did occur. Haussmann's wife, the gentle Octavie, once sighed: 'Every time a new work is started someone we know seems to become richer.'

Not so the Haussmanns. Despite industrious probing by would-be political assassins, not a franc among the billions invested by the city was found to have made its way into the prefect's pocket.

No doubt Georges-Eugène discussed with his boss a problem bound to arise with the 'alignment' of his new streets. The orderly profile that modern Paris

Right: Bandstands are a feature of many of the parks of Paris. Usually brightly painted iron posts support the roof, but this example is more rustic – in keeping with its artfully 'natural' setting – the Bois de Boulogne.

presents is due to its straight thoroughfares as well as to a decreed height of six storeys for all buildings. The wide avenues and low structures satisfied his passion for creating space and ventilation. At the same time they threatened to produce a monotonous cityscape. The solution Haussmann found soon became a hallmark of Paris – trees. He preferred chestnut trees, not only for their hardiness but also for their beauty – especially as they blossomed – some white, some pink – in April and May. Along the widest avenues, such as the Champs Elysées, double, sometimes triple, rows of trees were planted, while only a single row bordered the narrower arteries.

One grand thoroughfare remains treeless. Charles Garnier, the architect who built the new opera house, was adamant. Nothing, not even one tree, was to spoil the vista along the Avenue de l'Opéra which leads directly to, and frames, the magnificent building that was to became known as the Palais Garnier. And that's the way the avenue, paradoxically naked, remains to this day.

But Haussmann did not create broad, straight avenues simply because they were handsome, which they are, nor just to aereate the city, which they did. Their primary function was to get traffic, vehicular and pedestrian, moving. His intolerance of poor transport went back to his early years in Paris. It was reinforced by the lamentable condition of the inter-city routes he was forced to travel. But it was the little city of Nérac that first offered him the opportunity to take action. And to Georges-Eugène Haussmann, taking action was what life was all about.

Right: Most visitors, and many Parisians themselves, have little awareness of the nineteen small and less-small green spaces Haussmann tucked away throughout the city. One of the medium-size parks is that of the attractive Square de Batignolles in the 17th Arrondissement, shown here.

2
MOBILITY

PART 1

Nérac, 1832. Ostensibly Haussmann chose to reach Nérac by routing himself indirectly through Paris in order, he claimed, to avoid the worst of the mountain passes. However, the stage-coach was even less comfortable than the one that had taken him to Yssingeaux. Elegantly named the 'Diligence of Royal Messengers', the vehicle was not built for passengers of Georges-Eugène's bulk. Squeezed into a corner over the rear axle, he braced himself against the jolts and lurches of uniformly bad roads. Dust, heat and poor meals in questionable inns completed his misery. Three days later he reached the capital, muscles aching and legs swollen. In truth, his decision to visit Paris probably was not entirely based on considerations of comfort: drawing close to the sources of power always served as a tonic for Georges-Eugène Haussmann. During this visit he had the satisfaction of being at the Ministry of the Interior when an impassioned message arrived from Le Puy – a final plea to cancel his transfer to Nérac. Signed by a counsellor-of-state, the letter carried weight, though not enough to change matters:

'Within a few months (Haussmann) restored the region's lost loyalty to the government. He rallied the good citizens and reduced the others to silence.' Chaos, the counsellor concluded, would return with the departure of the sub-prefect. (Apparently this was not the case.) Once again Haussmann's stock notched up. With this kind of publicity, what young man could avoid arousing jealousy? Certainly not Haussmann whose opinions of his immediate bosses were seldom flattering or kept secret.

This is not to say that he lacked political skills – quite the reverse. Despite his constant nagging for promotion, he handled himself rather well in his relations with people of rank; he clearly regarded himself as a junior member of the club and he was treated accordingly. Certainly the support of his schoolmate, the Duc d'Orléans, next in line to the throne, did nothing to diminish their cordiality.

Left: The Rue du Croissant, near the Paris Bourse (Stock Exchange), typical of many streets as they appeared before the reconstruction of the city.

Having polished his contacts in the ministry, Georges-Eugène prepared to head south-west. Before he left Paris, however, he found time to visit Versailles for a talk with an admired uncle, Louis Haussmann, who had become mayor of the city. His contributions included improvements in local transport – a subject much on his nephew's mind after his recent journey. More generally, the two saw their profession from the same perspective – as an opportunity to bring order and efficiency into public administration.

Lumbering finally toward Nérac, Haussmann was dismayed to find that the roads of the region were in an even more lamentable state than those that had brought him to Paris. No direct connection to Nérac existed, as he knew. What he did not expect took place almost within sight of his destination. The road ended abruptly at the Garonne and the coach had to make a lengthy detour to arrive at a ferry.

Anyone who knew Haussmann could have gauged the depth of his disgust. Even as a student he had resented the labyrinth of meandering streets that stood

between his home and the university. Just as his revered school teacher, M. Legal, espoused a pragmatic approach to learning, Georges-Eugène adopted a direct approach to life; to get from one point to another, a straight line was best. The romantic ideas of his literary school-mate, de Musset, held less charm for him than the unvarnished prose of his family's notary. To learn first-hand that the national transportation system was no more efficient than that of Paris was not only disillusioning; it was infuriating.

Thus the newly appointed sub-prefect for Nérac arrived at his station in a foul mood. He even resolved to write to Paris next day to demand an immediate re-assignment. That, however, was before dining at his hotel. The meal was superb, rivalling anything Paris could offer. Never one to spurn fine food and vintage wines, he decided over coffee to scout out his new domain before acting rashly.

Left: This remarkable scene, perhaps from an operetta, shot in 1860 by an early photographic process called 'collodion', shows women unable to board a filled bus. One source of their frustration: the top deck was embargoed to them lest an ankle might show as they mounted the stairs.

Then the rains came. The streets of the town turned into quagmires. Haussmann's boots and trousers were encrusted with mud thrown up by horses' hooves. None the less he completed his tour of inspection, hoping to find at least one or two paved roads. Convinced finally that his quest was in vain, he returned to the hotel, all thoughts of requesting a re-assignment forgotten. A firm resolution took their place; when the time came for him to leave Nérac, the townspeople would be walking on paved streets! Likewise the other 66 communes under his authority would be linked by proper roads. Haussmann had become Haussmann, a crusader for mobility.

The problems he encountered, as well as their solution, might also be called 'Haussmannian'. For example, he soon learned that there was no money in the treasury to underwrite such an important programme. He promptly resurrected a forgotten municipal statute that required male citizens to contribute a portion of their time to the maintenance of the public services. But Georges-Eugène proclaimed that he was not one to be unreasonable about the application of this ancient regulation; those affected could discharge their obligation by making cash payments to the commune.

No doubt Haussmann knew he was on shaky legal ground. But the work got under way; after all, wasn't his action clearly in the public interest? Later on, he could fret about small points of propriety. Luckily, his fiscal creativity was never tested in court; the national administration soon decreed a local tax to help communities finance public improvements.

'Never', wrote Haussmann later, 'did a vote in *parlement* give me greater satisfaction.' No longer would he be forced to rely on romantic methods of raising money.

Not for the first time, or the last, Haussmann displayed more enthusiasm for getting on with projects than for getting along with his boss. An accomplished courtier when he wished to be, the sub-prefect repeatedly broke two rules sacred to the civil service. He jumped the chain of command by going over the head of the prefect, situated in Agen, only eighteen miles to the north-west, and he often neglected to render a report of his activities. These sins were scarlet enough, but, just as offensive, he socialised only with people he wanted to cultivate. And that clearly did not include the prefect. A mover and shaker, Haussmann sometimes moved too fast and too often shook the sensibilities of habit-bound residents.

The first signs of a schism with the prefect can be found in their comments on each other. Haussmann, according to his boss, should use 'more tact, be less aloof and show more consideration for the wisdom of influential citizens'. This report to headquarters goes on to express the hope that 'Georges-Eugène will come to understand better his role, as well as the little niceties of dealing with the local population'.*

From his point of view, Haussmann assessed the prefect as 'a hard worker, master of all the unimportant details of administration – far more a bureaucrat than an executive'.

Such a mutual lack of appreciation could only move their relationship from bad to worse – and in time it did.

Meanwhile Haussmann found himself in his element. The network of paved roads was spreading and construction had started on an essential bridge. In terms of his personal life, Nérac offered him the comfort of being in a Protestant centre – one that could even claim to have given sanctuary to Calvin. On a less spiritual plane, the young women of Nérac and their mothers were very aware of the presence of the dynamic young sub-prefect whose elegant figure was everywhere to be seen. And still a bachelor! Haussmann claimed to be annoyed by speculation about his plans to terminate his presumed sad and lonely mode of existence. Actually he had an attractive apartment in the Hôtel de Ville where he was served by an excellent cook and his wife. Above all, he was deep into his crusade for civic improvement, which was soon to involve him in a second crusade – to set off an explosion in public education. All in all, he was able to put up with the fact that, through no fault of his own, he tended to make women sigh.

Just as his life was settling into a well-ordered pattern, a visitor from Paris arrived one morning to ask for his help. George Sand, the celebrated cigar-smoking novelist, had come to Nérac to reclaim her daughter, Solange, who, she asserted, had been abducted by Sand's ex-husband. In little Nérac, she created a stir by appearing, as usual, in a man's clothes. She carried a letter from Georges-Eugène's top boss, the Minister of the Interior, authorising the sub-prefect to act in any way 'practicable' to recover the child. At this time Sand was at the height of her fame and notoriety, but for the moment her mind was totally with her daughter.

In Haussmann's lexicon, 'action' meant direct action. Helping Sand into his carriage, he ordered the driver to speed to the nearby château where Solange was being held. On arrival, the sub-prefect sent in orders for the father, a baron, to present himself. Wealth, rank, châteaux – nothing could faze an aroused Haussmann. Within minutes Solange leapt into the carriage and the arms of her mother.

'Madame,' said the baron, 'I have no choice but to yield to the violent

---

* Jean des Cars. *Haussmann: La Gloire du Second Empire.* Perrin, Paris, 1978

Above: The Arc de Triomphe, completed in 1836 to honour Napoleon I, the uncle of Napoleon III. The prefect made it the hub of twelve radiating avenues leading to other hubs – one of the all-time marvels of city planning.

measures you are taking against me.'

'Monsieur,' Sand replied, 'I have never refused to allow you to see your daughter, but you chose to carry her off. You force me to pattern my actions after your own.'

Despite the excellent chef at the local inn, Haussmann could not bring himself to install mother and daughter in public lodgings. Instead he turned over the best rooms of his residence to them. There followed a round of dinners to introduce the celebrated author to local personages. After they left, she and Georges-Eugène had long talks, mostly about philosophy. Politics was barred; both knew that there could be no meeting-ground there. Sand was obviously pleased to encounter so far from Paris a Parisian so cultivated and well informed.

'He was a serious person,' she later wrote, 'eager to talk about general problems, but his sense of discrimination prevented him from raising questions that might be considered indelicate.'

They parted friends, she inviting him to her country home, Nohant, where she received the most famous writers, artists and musicians of the day.

The visit never materialised, but how could Haussmann foretell that the time would come when he would find George Sand among his supporters as he set about creating a new Paris?

Among the shortcomings of the county for which Haussmann was responsible, he ranked illiteracy almost as deplorable as poor roads. When at last Paris passed a law to underwrite public schooling at the elementary level, probably no one rejoiced more than the sub-prefect of Nérac whose own thirst for knowledge was insatiable. Though not yet obligatory, schooling was now made available to those who wished it. As to whether this or that particular school was to be church or state controlled, Georges-Eugène refused to become embroiled. To him, what mattered was to take the first giant step to reduce the number of illiterates in France.

Once again Haussmann set off on campaign, his limitless energy igniting enthusiasm throughout the area. Not only did he work with local authorities in selecting the sites for schools, but he even concerned himself with such matters as their furnishings. He joined the meetings of committees for the selection of teachers and to fix their salaries. In listing first admissions he favoured children from the poorest families. Finally, before the autumn of 1835, at least one school had been established in every important community.

In Paris, the Minister of Education found himself intrigued by a map showing the dense concentration of new schools in the sub-prefecture of Nérac. No area in south-west France could compare. He asked who was the sub-prefect of the county. Jotting down the name Haussmann, he resolved to pass it along to the Minister of the Interior. Somehow, in the unceasing jousting for power so endemic within the administration, his good intention seems to have been lost.

Nevertheless, not long afterwards, Georges-Eugène learned that he was being recommended to receive the Order of the Légion d'honneur. This was an exceptional distinction for someone only 28 years old. In his mind, it even took precedence over the medal he'd won in the three-day revolution. While it wouldn't be correct to say that Haussmann performed in order to receive such rewards, it's clear that he relished them inordinately as validation of his own assessment of his abilities. But then there was his grumpy superior in Agen. Apparently he was responsible for holding up the actual bestowal of the award for a full three years.

The summer of 1837 marked the beginning of a giant upsurge in the economy of France as well as in the mobility of its citizens. The railway had arrived. The celebration in nearby Bordeaux of the first passenger service in France, linking the city with Paris, was an occasion that Haussmann – with his passion for improved transport – didn't want to miss.

As it turned out, the same visit would revolutionise his own life. Through an old friend, Henri Laharpe, he was introduced to the Laharpe family. His friend's sister, Octavie, had turned down a number of suitors because of her desire to care for her ageing parents. This was so unlike the huntresses of Nérac that Haussmann found it easy to talk to her. One year later they were married. In 19th-century provincial France, this was viewed as a lightning courtship.

It was a good marriage. Haussmann described Octavie as 'friendly, gracious and even pretty'. Moreover her family, Protestant and of Swiss origin, had profited handsomely in the Bordeaux wine business. Although she was two years older than her husband, that presented no problem at the time. (The same could not be said later on.)

Octavie was a knowledgeable hostess but she could hardly have been prepared for a royal visit only two weeks after she moved to Nérac. The Duc d'Orléans,

Right: In 1857 city of Paris took possession of some horse-drawn buse owned by several companies. Until then, the buses ra only on profitable routes. Haussman insisted they serve neighbourhoods. F the first time, Parisians could circulate through the city for entertainment, shopping or, simpl sightseeing. This i in front of the Ga de l'Est, the easte railway station, s the biggest buses, called the 'Impériales'.

Haussmann's former classmate and heir to the throne, was to visit Bordeaux. The sub-prefect's invitation to the royal couple to stay with the newly-weds was promptly accepted despite the enormous difference in rank. One reason might have been that the duchess also was a Lutheran. Evidently the visit was successful for on his departure the duke whispered to his protégé: 'Before long you'll have your prefecture.' Haussmann's goal was in sight.

However, a new prefect was now in charge of the *département* that included Nérac. What remained unchanged was the rising tension between prefect and headstrong subordinate. It was the duke's visit that brought matters to the boil. M. Brun, the current prefect, was furious that Haussmann had seized the initiative, without consultation, to entertain the duke. The time had passed for slaps on the wrist. Instead very tough messages flew – one addressed to Haussmann inviting him 'never to ignore the rules of the hierarchy' – meaning, 'don't talk to Paris without talking to me first'. Another missive was a stern report to the ministry, listing Haussmann's sins. Among the phrases it contained were 'insolent', 'questionable character', 'succumbs to his prejudices and dislikes', 'warps facts'. Interestingly, M. Brun also complained of an absence of 'social contact' with this supposedly dubious character. Jealousy and wounded pride seem largely to have guided the prefect's pen. He was accurate, however, in his portrayal of an independent, ambitious young career officer.

Haussmann was able to brush off this unpleasantness because of his conviction that his promotion to another *département* was pending. After all, he had the duke's word for it.

For once he had miscalculated. When his orders finally came through, they staggered him. They contained nothing resembling a promotion; quite the

— Allons bon ! encore le baron Haussmann !

Left: Published 30 years ago in the newspaper Figaro, *this cartoon was one of a series on historical figures. A liberal translation would be: 'Here we go again. It's the Baron Haussmann', a caustic reminder of the number of people forced to find new lodgings because of the demolition of old buildings.*

reverse: once again he was being exiled to a small town, this time in the foothills of the Pyrenees close to the border with Spain. A slap in the face! If there could be any doubt about that, the accompanying message removed it. 'The good of the service does not permit you to remain in your present post. We [the ministry] regret that we cannot put your personal convenience ahead of the interest of the administration.'

A chill wind blew from Paris. Meanwhile, only a month earlier, at her family home in Bordeaux, Octavie had given birth to a daughter, Marie-Henriette. She was preparing her return to Nérac when the bombshell landed. How could any man ask a young mother who so loved her parents, to move with their new-born child to the mountainous wilds of the Franco–Spanish frontier?

Speaking far and wide of his 'disgrace', Georges-Eugène made up his mind to resign. First he took off for Paris to confront the Minister of the Interior. There he stumbled into yet another change of administration which once again had swept friends back into power. They managed to convince him that the assignment to the St-Girons sub-prefecture was far more than a routine transfer. First, the work to be accomplished was of international importance. Secondly, it would be of short duration if he was successful in his mission.

And the mission? Arms were being smuggled across the border from France to Spanish revolutionaries, the Carlists, badly damaging relations between the two countries. St-Girons was the sluice through which the contraband passed. The government required a strong man to flush out the smugglers and put an end to the traffic.

Right: Haussmann was cruelly attacked by the political enemies of Napoleon III. This contemporary cartoon shows him as a beaver, destroying and rebuilding for his own profit. In fact, he died without resources after refusing a pension from the government.

LA MÉNAGERIE IMPÉRIALE.

HAUSSMANN.

N°8

Haussmann half suspected officialdom was sugar-coating a blunder, but his suspicions had melted by the time he was to leave Paris. He was received by the president of the royal council, the grave Thiers, who personally wished him well in his mission. In good humour that night, the president even laughed at a little joke – something almost unheard of in his governmental circles.

Then from the prime minister himself came a letter thanking Georges-Eugène for his 'acceptance of this sacrifice which places the administration under an obligation I shall not fail to honour ...'

So the government was testing his strength before assigning him to higher responsibilities! Or so Georges-Eugène reasoned. He tore up the resignation he'd written and returned to collect his baggage at Nérac where Octavie was preparing herself and Marie-Henriette to rejoin her family at Bordeaux.

Haussmann was leaving a Nérac and its surrounding communities that had been transformed during his eight years. Paved roads linked the principal centres, traffic was moving over his bridge, a newly surfaced highway led to the prefecture at Agen. And, throughout the county, children were being schooled in the hopes of a far brighter future than their parents had known.

He was also leaving behind many wounded feelings and outright enemies who had opposed his high-handed methods. Prominent among these was his boss, prefect Brun. Unfortunately, no one had yet found a way to teach Haussmann respect for leaders who worshipped at the altar of organisational hierarchy.

Georges-Eugène spent little time with Octavie and the baby. The quicker he tracked down the arms smugglers, the sooner he would return to accept the promotion he was certain would be awaiting him.

PART 2

Paris, 1858. At first the sound was that of light hail striking a metal roof. Then, as the noise rose, the crowd knew the ceremony was about to begin. The clatter of 400 horses' hooves soon mingled with the cheers of tens of thousands of Parisians. Over a stretch of two kilometres, they packed the pavements of the new Boulevard de Sébastopol. An immense curtain stretching across the entire width of the road swept open. At that moment the avenue was joined to the Boulevard de Strasbourg. From the junction of the two, looming to the north, could be seen the façade of the Gare de l'Est, the eastern rail gateway to Paris.

Trumpets sounded, drums rolled and the Emperor, at the head of a hundred lancers, passed through. Then came the open landau carrying a resplendent Empress Eugénie towards the speaker's stand. There Georges-Eugène Haussmann, prefect of the Seine, awaited the imperial couple.

No one was surprised that Haussmann made a graceful speech of welcome; by then he was practised in the art. What was unprecedented was the response from the Emperor; he publicly gave full credit to Haussmann and his team for the successful completion of the work after five years of effort. To be sure, other streets had been inaugurated before – the Rue de Rivoli, the Avenue Victoria, the Avenue de Strasbourg. But this one eclipsed all of them in terms of magnificence. On either side the dark, tawdry streets of the old Paris seemed to cringe in the light and air that suddenly swept through the neighbourhood.

To take pride in his accomplishments was hardly foreign to Georges-Eugène's nature. What must have brought him close to ecstasy was this benediction before tens of thousands of Parisians, among them hundreds of notables, by the most popular ruler of France since Napoleon I. He publicly gave full credit to the prefect and his team for the results of his first five years of achievement. Georges-Eugène's childhood dream of becoming a page to the Emperor Napoleon I had been surpassed by reality. Instead, he was now revealed as one of the most valued lieutenants of another Napoleon. And, obviously, this Napoleon had found in his prefect the key to his own dream, to rule from a city that would become recognised as the glory of Europe.

Other recognition was not long in coming. One prominent general opined: 'This type of artery must be imposed on all parts of Paris. It represents a model of urbanism of the Second Empire, both in its structural technique and in its architecture.'

The Boulevard de Strasbourg and the Boulevard de Sébastopol together formed the principal north-south thoroughfare of Paris. The meandering Seine provided a sort of east-west artery. It was already so clogged with shipping that Haussmann was forced to impose strict navigational controls just to keep the traffic moving. To do so involved him in one of many disputes with the prefect of Paris who considered the river to be a part of his jurisdiction. As usual Haussmann won the row by appealing to his boss.

Even before Napoleon I, rulers had been intrigued by the creation of what came to be called 'the great crossroads of Paris'. While the two new boulevards formed the northern part of the cross, it had yet to cross the Seine to the left bank. The east-west axis by land remained to be created. Haussmann's first street-clearing marked a start; it extended the Rue de Rivoli to his Hôtel de Ville and there linked up with an enlarged Rue St-Antoine. Even after the accomplishment of this work, however, both extremities stopped far short of the eastern and western edges of the city.

Haussmann was to devote the next twelve years of his life to the enormous challenge of opening up the city. His opponents, always ready with a barb, came up with a nickname: *'Haussmann, l'Eventreur'*, foreshadowing London's 'Jack the Ripper', because of the number of demolitions he ordered.

The arteries created by *'La Grande Croisée'* (the great crossroads) were to form, literally, the central circulation system for the Paris-to-be. From it would spring a series of hubs distributed around the city, with spokes leading from each centre of activity to others. Within the whole complex structure, Haussmann and the Emperor also designed a circular pattern; traffic would flow from the centre of the cross (Place du Châtelet) on the right bank across the present Concorde bridge to the left bank and then return to the right bank via the bridge which would be called the Pont de Sully.

below: With the transformation of the Bois de Boulogne, Napoleon III demanded an elegant approach to the new park; the Avenue Foch, shown here, was Haussmann's superb answer. Originally named 'Avenue de l'Impératrice' to honour the Empress Eugénie, it became the route travelled by visiting royalty to reach the Arc de Triomphe, from which this photograph is taken.

Throughout the years of reconstruction, a mystery remains: whence came the apparently inexhaustible sources of Haussmann's energy? Not only did he bear the ultimate responsibility for commanding 14,000 workers, but he found himself constantly required to defend himself against a myriad of enemies – political, aesthetic, personal and the aggrieved who were forced out of their homes by his programme of demolition. Then, too, Haussmann's routine included more than the vast spectrum of activity linked to the rebuilding of Paris. He was impresario for holiday celebrations on a truly imperial scale as well as official host to visiting heads of state who, as they do to this day, must be received with honours at the Hôtel de Ville. Almost from the first day as prefect, he had a battalion of workmen clearing the area around the handsome building – itself nothing less than a palace – to give it a proper setting. Soon Octavie joined him and, retiring though she was by nature, found herself cast in the role of official hostess of Paris. Never seeking to be a grand star, she played her part well. In time there were few European potentates she had not welcomed to Paris.

Georges-Eugene Haussmann's definition of 'receiving' was as expansive as his thoughts on rebuilding. More often than not, his idea of a reception was a dinner for 100 followed by a ball. From his days in Bordeaux, under the tutelage of M. Laharpe, he had acquired an almost professional knowledge of wines. As a result, his cellar in Paris was reputed to be the finest in France.

The cuisine at the Hôtel de Ville was worthy of the wines. A typical banquet might consist of shrimp soup, stuffed quail, slices of beef in a savoury sauce, carp and tender asparagus – all followed by an equally impressive array of cheeses and sweets.

'To remain awake after that, exercise was essential. Leading the quadrille, of course, was Georges-Eugène. One newspaper reported that the Hôtel de Ville had become 'a palace of legend, the product of the imagination of poets'.

Such opulent productions were staged not only for Haussmann's pleasure; they were an integral part of the Emperor's determination to make Paris shine more brilliantly than any other city of Europe. Once the candles were snuffed, the prefect could be found at his desk on the ground floor, preparing for the day to come. He would be up, ready for action, at 7.30 in winter, 6.30 in summer.

One of the challenges confronting him was how to integrate the little-

Below: The Sully bridge over the Seine. This bridge is the only one not constructed at a right-angle to the river. Typical of his passion for noble perspectives, Haussman ordered the bridge to be canted so as to produce views of two monuments at once, this one looking south toward the Panthéon, the other looking north toward the 'Column of July'.

developed western edge of the city into the creation of the great crossing. At this time the western edge of urban Paris was marked by Louis XV's Place de la Concorde where so many aristocrats, scholars and scientists had ascended the steps to the guillotine during the Revolution. Beyond that the Champs Elysées was not much more than a rustic swathe leading upwards to the magnificent Arc de Triomphe, constructed 23 years before Haussmann took office. He and the Emperor, whose uncle the arch celebrated, decided that it would become a major focal point in the system of streets and avenues they were creating throughout Paris.

The decision illustrates a fact about Paris that sets it apart from any other world capital. Nearly always the hubs of circulation that Haussmann created rotated about the core of a *quartier* that was already an important centre of activity. At the same time we find that, more often than not, the neighbourhood itself was identified by an already existing monument. The location of the hubs was therefore chosen largely because of the visibility of such landmarks. The Place de la Bastille and the Place de la République are typical.

Below: Looking north from the Sully bridge, one sees the column commemorating the fall of the Bourbon monarchy.

The alignment of the Champs Elysées with the Louvre Palace, the Arch of the Carrousel and Haussmann's Place de l'Etoile form what is generally thought to be the most spectacular civic panorama in the world. The concept of the Etoile alone was breathtaking, even in terms of the outsized imagination of Haussmann. Radiating from the arch he added seven grand avenues which, with the existing five, joined to form the star that gave the circle its name. Like the hour-hand of a giant

clock, each exit points towards another centre. Noon carries one towards the Porte Maillot, six o'clock to the Place de la Concorde, 15 minutes after the hour to the Place des Ternes, 45 minutes to the Place du Trocadéro. Only the Avenue Carnot, at five past twelve, eventually straggles off into a limbo of undistinguished buildings; the original plan for its extension would have carried it to what is now the junction of the Avenue de Villiers and the ring of outer boulevards.

The architect, Hittorff, well recovered from the shock of Haussmann's explosive reception of his plan for the Avenue de l'Impératrice (now Avenue Foch), situated at five minutes before the hour, now had another opportunity to exercise his skill. At first his low-profile buildings that encircled the Place de l'Etoile were spurned by critics because of their modest height. Yet this is exactly what reveals the architect's genius. Because of Hittorff's restraint no high-profile structures detract from the sheer grandeur of the monument. Haussmann's triple rows of plane trees further shielded the arch from the possibility of conflict with its neighbours.

By day the sounds of pickaxes, crashing walls and the neighing of overworked wagon-horses filled the air. At night also there was no surcease. Haussmann had discovered the magic of electricity. He never did accept its use for street-lighting, but after sundown the glare of electric arcs cast an eerie illumination over the cavities and half-standing walls that now scarred entire neighbourhoods. Even rational citizens, who accepted the need for modernisation, became alarmed at the desolation, convinced that the prefect was determined to level the entire city. This was by no means the case. What he sought was not to destroy, except where necessary,

Below: Haussmann tripled the size of the Place de la République, in order to make it the hub of nine boulevards and avenues, most of them created under his regime. The Place is to eastern Paris what the Etoile, with its twelve intersecting steets, is to the west side. Underground are the platforms of six Métro lines.

Right: The same approach to the Place de la République today. Without Haussmann's broad avenues, Paris would long ago have been strangled by snarled traffic.

but to open up Paris – primarily to help people live decently and to move from one place to another without frustration or fear. Nevertheless, many joined those who fervently wished Haussmann had chosen music as his career. Others wished the same thing – but for different reasons. 'Decent housing' did not mean housing for the poor but for the middle and upper classes. They foresaw, correctly, that Haussmann's gentrification of Paris would push the working-class population outside central Paris and into the suburbs.

One word tells much about Haussmann's thought process. The word is circulation – circulation of air, to be sure, but also an improved vehicular circulation that could come about only through the creation of broad, straight streets and avenues. He spurned the idea of traffic, which could be blocked (as it usually was); in contrast, circulation flowed.

One day a house collapsed under its own weight and age, killing an inhabitant. Haussmann's ever-present – and growing – Greek chorus of complainers charged that vibration from construction had undermined the building. Expert opinion, however, supported the prefect. Scores of people were doomed to die unless the city pressed forward with the destruction of buildings that had only one another for support.

The word 'gentrification' had not yet made its appearance. Had it existed, the opposition press certainly would have banalised it. The three successive reconstruction plans that finally brought 'Haussmannian' Paris into being ignored the poorer residential quarters beyond the Place de la Bastille. Thus the handsome

Parc de Vincennes on the eastern edge of Paris promptly came to be known as 'the poor people's park'. Likewise the Opéra de la Bastille was conceived a century-and-a-half later as 'the poor man's opera'. The phrase, however, turned sardonic once the price of tickets was announced.

In contrast to the eastern part of Paris, to the west colossal projects were under way, most notably around the Palais Royal, Notre-Dame Cathedral and the elegant Parc Monceau. Clearly Haussmann and Napoleon III were vulnerable to the charge that the poor were being chased from the centre of the city. In Paris the change was abrupt, whereas the affluent only gradually took over the centres of London and New York. Elsewhere many large industrial cities reversed the process; thanks to the automobile, the middle classes fled to the suburbs while the poor found themselves left behind in the inner cities.

Another charge, frequently repeated to this day, was less justified. Opponents of the regime convinced themselves, as well as others, that the wide, straight avenues, reflecting Haussmann's passion for the direct line, were designed to help the regime put down rebellions. It is obvious that troops could chase down rioters more readily if the insurgents could no longer take refuge behind barricades thrown up in dark alleys and crooked streets. One general was widely quoted as saying, 'Bullets don't know how to take the second turning to the left'. Another military man pondered the desirability of straightening out the curvaceous River Seine.

In fact, only two projects out of the hundreds undertaken seem to have been designed with military purposes in mind. Aside from its value as beautification and as an aid to circulation, the extension of the Rue de Rivoli eastward towards the Place de la Bastille cleared the route between the working man's district and the Hôtel de Ville, making it easier for troops to bar the way to insurgents marching towards the Place de la Concorde.

Left: The Avenue de l'Opéra was not completed until 1877, even though the work on the building began under Haussmann in 1862. The extent of the demolition necessary is shown in this contemporary photograph of the work on the final segment.

The one project clearly and exclusively intended to aid the police was in fact one of the most imaginative of all Haussmann's initiatives. Before Louis-Philippe became Emperor, the Canal of Saint Martin formed a natural defence line for rioters retreating to the eastern part of Paris. Through an audacious scheme, the prefect deprived them of their time-honoured fall-back position along the eastern bank of the waterway. He drained the canal, lowered its bed by 12 feet, then covered the canal with a central mall more than a kilometre long. Many pedestrians strolling along the resulting green belt today have no idea that barges and yachts are gliding along beneath their feet.

At the beginning of 1859 Paris was a city imprisoned behind two walls. The exterior wall consisted of a series of military fortifications. Their uselessness – to be demonstrated in pain and sorrow twelve years later – should have been enough to discourage the building of the Maginot Line in the 1930s; it was not. Nor was the inner wall the boon to the city it was intended to be. This barrier had been erected for the purpose of collecting taxes on food and merchandise entering the city. It too was doomed.

To someone of Haussmann's nature this imprisonment was unacceptable. Even at the cost of eventual tax losses, he and the Emperor decided to tear down the inner wall and to annex to the city of Paris the communities that stood between the two walls. Napoleon III signed a decree to this effect on 1 January 1859. Overnight the area of the city more than doubled while the population leapt by 32 per cent to 1,600,000. Instead of twelve *arrondissements*, or boroughs, there were (and are today) twenty.

Problems of integration inevitably followed, but they were overcome and soon circulation flowed freely between Paris and eighteen former suburbs – among them those bearing such famous names as Montmartre, Passy and Auteuil.

Right: Until 1860 all produce entering Paris was taxed. Three toll stations remain. This one, at the entrance to the Parc Monceau, existed to inspect products coming in from what was then the northern boundary of the city.

Perhaps the inhabitants of no city tolerate boredom less gracefully than Parisians. Within a few years after the stir caused by the creation of the Boulevard de Sébastopol, new thoroughfares were being opened so frequently as to become almost a matter of routine. Only two years later the Boulevard St-Michel completed the north-south axis of the great crossing which now spanned the Seine to link the hub at the Place du Châtelet with the left bank. There it pierced the centre of the student quarter to approach the hub of Denfert-Rochereau where the new Boulevards Raspail and Arago, and the present Avenue du Général Leclerc and Avenue René Coty all converge.

However, the excitement surrounding the opening of major new streets had not yet quite ebbed four years after the dedication of the Boulevard de Sébastopol. The inauguration of the Boulevard Malesherbes in 1862 turned out to be an occasion even more colourful. For one thing, the project represented a very visible high point in the transformation of Paris. Another less obvious reason lay close to the heart of the Emperor. With his nostalgia for England, he was enthralled also by the destination of the new thoroughfare. Rising from the Place de la Madeleine, the boulevard led directly to the plain of Monceau. There Napoleon III had caused an entirely different kind of Paris to be constructed. His instructions to Haussmann had been, in effect: 'Let us create a neighbourhood of smaller, more intimate buildings, one that will be reminiscent of the Mayfair district of London.' His idea was, needless to say, carried out. Built around the posh Parc Monceau, the *quartier* fails, however, to capture the British cosiness that Napoleon III wistfully sought. The stamp 'Made in France' is everywhere – especially in the romantic park itself with its replica of Roman ruins, waterfalls and carefully trimmed grass on which the richest kids of Paris are forbidden to tread.

None the less, the opening of the Boulevard Malesherbes was trumpeted as a great occasion. The adjective 'great' was well justified; the street itself is one of the most impressive in Paris. Its construction turned out to be particularly challenging because of the need to tame a sharp rise of the terrain. Begun under Napoleon I, the work had progressed only 200 metres during the 50 years before Haussmann threw his force behind it. Now it stretched $1\frac{1}{2}$ kilometres northwards.

Haussmann seized the inaugural ceremony to counter-attack the frequent charges that the transformation of Paris was carried out only for the benefit of the rich. 'Our work is destined more to improve the lives of the less-favoured class than to benefit the others,' he proclaimed. Then his combative nature took over: 'Unfortunately, no one is aware of this fact because the writers and the talkers seldom stray from their expensive neighbourhoods to see what is being done to improve the housing of ordinary citizens.' The statement is typical of Haussmann's dangerous habit of airing exactly what he thought. He needed a public-relations agent, but unfortunately the profession had not yet been invented.

On this occasion Napoleon III praised Haussmann with more than words. In full view of all of the dignitaries of Paris, he announced that his prefect was awarded the Grand Cross of Légion d'honneur, the highest decoration of the order. Then he rode off on horseback to examine the famous golden gates of the

Above: The Avenue de l'Opéra as seen from the Louvre Palace. It is one of the few important Paris streets bereft of trees. The architect Garnier wanted it that way in order to preserve unobstructed the view of his masterpiece, the Paris opera house.

Parc Monceau – the most expensive portals in Europe – and the nearby construction that was fast replacing a barren plain dotted with huts and shanties.

At least in the matter of public transport, Haussmann made good his claim that his work was improving the quality of life for the ordinary citizen. He hadn't long been in office when he foresaw that his new avenues would revolutionise the habits of the people. No longer would they be prisoners of their neighbourhood. Instead they were being freed to move from one part of the city to another. Clearly, getting about on foot would have to be supplemented by decent wheeled transport.

Omnibuses were in service, but they were controlled by eleven separate companies. Their lines ran through the most populated areas so as to pack in a maximum number of passengers and profit. Haussmann resolved to change that. He mapped out a city-wide service that would transport passengers, according to their real needs, to and from all parts of the city. To bring this about, he had to wrest control of the companies from their owners. This was accomplished through a decree signed by the Emperor. Armed with this signature, Georges-Eugène undertook an added responsibility – for an organisation owning more than 3,000 horses and nearly 600 buses. In itself, the role was important enough to carry the title of chief executive officer.

Forging this sprawling entity into a rational system of transport dramatically altered the pattern of daily life in Paris. Now a person living in one district could work in another, and entertainment was available to audiences coming from all parts of the city. The advantages of freedom to circulate had become available to everyone.

The mobility of women, however, was restricted; they were not permitted to climb to the upper deck of the vehicles; the danger was too great that they might expose an ankle.

In 1861 the Emperor granted additional powers to his prefect, giving him the right to approve or disapprove the decisions of certain city authorities. Oddly, the action was the result of the first setback Haussmann had experienced in his steady accretion of power. He had already been authorised to attend the meetings of the imperial council, the key governing body of twelve

Above: The Rue d'Auteuil carries the name of one of the communities annexed by the city of Paris under Napoleon III and Haussmann. in 1860. Photographed in 1999, the scene would have been little changed if taken by the photographer Marville at the time of annexation.

ministers over which Napoleon III presided. This was an unprecedented honour to be bestowed on a 'mere' prefect. In fact, the title itself now irritated Georges-Eugène. He felt he had every right to the called 'Minister of Paris'. Haussmann proposed the change to the Emperor who apparently floated the idea before his council of ministers. It was not well received so Louis Napoleon let the matter drop, substituting instead the piecemeal delegation of authority stipulated in the decree he finally signed. For the first time he failed to stand behind his lieutenant; he may have felt, correctly, that he would soon be facing other, more critical issues. In fact, the compromise in itself made clear that his authority already was being chipped away by the opposition.

For the moment, however, both he and his protégé had reached a kind of apogee. Georges-Eugène even struck back at the recalcitrant ministers. He pointed out that the prefect of the Seine was not a prefect like the others because Paris was not a city like others. 'I am not ambitious. In my place, an ambitious man would ... have negotiated with certain interests that I've encountered along the way and that I've never hesitated to cold-shoulder, no matter what the risk. An ambitious man would not commit such folly. Everyone knows how I've never measured my hours of rest.' An ambitious man would take better care of himself. Instead of seeking repose, he had better things to do. Those precious hours he preferred to spend day and night at the service of the state.

Once again, he spoke the truth. As usual, he stated his case in terms of self-flattery that others often found infuriating. We could add that an 'ambitious man' would not have done that. He welcomed medals and honours as recognition of his accomplishments, but he sought power in order to get on with his job. It meant freedom to make decisions with the least possible interference from rival bureaucrats. Of these there were many, and many of them were small-minded people.

Circulation – of air, people, vehicles represented a large part of that job.

But there remained another kind of circulation that was desperately restricted – the flow of water into and out of the city. In this matter, the enemy was far more to be dreaded than the attack of any politician.

Its name was cholera.

3
❖
WATER

April 1840. Sub-prefect Haussmann arrived in St-Girons with the same lack of enthusiasm that he had felt for his two previous posts. None such were likely, he knew, to make full use of his abilities. As always, he saw his proper role to be that of a prefect without the 'sub'. Nothing less would grant him the kind of responsibility he knew was capable of handling.

But once again, he soon found himself captivated by the job at hand – especially by two elements. One was the rugged façade of the Pyrenees that soared two thousand metres above St-Girons to mark the frontier between France and Spain. In those forests and ravines, hidden from his gaze, lurked his quarry, the arms smugglers. But directly under his eyes thundered cascades of crystalline water released by the snowy crests of the mountains.

All his passion for cleanliness, all his desire to wash away the pollution of the dirty city that was Paris, surfaced from the artesian depths of his being. He needed only a day to learn that water provided whatever power was required by St-Girons's modest industries. And not much later he stumbled on the intriguing fact that the health-giving qualities of the water varied with the geology of the area through which it coursed.

To be sure, the routine paper work of the sub-prefecture got done, but not with zest. Obviously Georges-Eugène regarded his stay in St-Girons as little more than a pause while he awaited a more important assignment. One clear indication was the location of his office. On arrival he discovered that the living quarters of the building that officially housed the sub-prefecture contained no furnishings. Instead of ordering what was needed, he rented three rooms in the Hôtel de France, where he had checked in, and there set up his command post.

As at Yssingeaux, Georges-Eugène spent more time in the saddle than in his so-called office. His mission was to close the border between France and Spain in order to thwart the passage of arms to Spanish revolutionaries seeking to replace the queen by her brother, Don Carlos. Eager to preserve good relations with a legitimate monarch across the border, the French government was determined to erase any appearance of support for the Carlists. (The situation was not very different from France's co-operation today with Spain in its fight against the Basque separatists.)

Haussmann determined to scout out the situation first-hand. Accompanied by the local captain of the frontier guard, he traced and retraced the mountain trails that led upward from St-Girons. The pair were outdoors in good weather and bad, and they remained in the open many nights as well as days. Night-time was the most dangerous. Unarmed, the two men lay half-awake, using their saddles as pillows, straining to hear footsteps or voices. They were threatened by both man and the bears that roamed the mountains. Smugglers might stumble upon them in the dark and the bears could be attracted by the smell of their freshly cooked fish. To beat off intruders, human or animal, they each had a couple of iron staves.

It was late spring and melting snow made the rocky slopes treacherous beneath the horses' hooves. Yet on occasion Haussmann and his companion worked their way up to the highest passes, 8,000 feet and more above sea level. At the higher elevations, snow still lay on the ground, sometimes knee-deep. This could be a help rather than a hindrance; imprints in the snow marked the presence of their quarry.

Before long, Haussmann was able to size up the situation. Clearly such a manhunt was too much for two men to deal with. At the same time, word had reached St-Girons that relations between France and Spain were becoming increasingly delicate. Paris wanted action. The sub-prefect promptly mounted a kind of operation well known to frontier sheriffs in the USA. He recruited armed posses of forest rangers and local police, and stationed them across the strategic routes used by the smugglers. Haussmann himself co-ordinated the operation, riding from post to post to make sure of their vigilance and to pass and receive information.

To his surprise, the sub-prefect found himself enjoying his rugged job and even rather liking St-Girons where bear-cubs played in the streets with the town's

Below: The reservoir of the Parc Montsouris, along with that of Menilmontant, marked the end of a ten-year struggle by Haussmann to obtain financing to bring pure water by aqueduct into Paris. His victory ended the waves of cholera that over the centuries had resulted in the deaths of tens of thousands of Parisians.

children and the canine population. As summer arrived, Octavie joined him. She relished the rounded beauty of the foothills and together they sampled the good things to eat and drink which the area had to offer. Perhaps her sole source of anxiety was the obvious danger faced by her husband in carrying out his mission. Georges-Eugène's loyal groom vowed that he would never dare to return Haussmann's horse to her without its rider.

The sub-prefect found more of interest in St-Girons than food and wine. He was to write later: 'The county of St-Girons offered me an excellent field of research for my studies, seriously begun years ago, on the interesting subject of water from the point of view of its health-giving qualities.' He soon discovered that the incidence of goitre in a nearby valley in the Bellongue area was sufficiently high to attract the interest of the national health authorities. The chief researcher, brought in from Lyon, thought that the problem arose from the rich foliage of the trees abundant in the locality; he supposed that it interfered with a proper circulation of air and thus affected the quality of the water.

Haussmann disagreed. He noted that the river that watered the particular valley where the abnormalities were found passed over layers of stratified slate. These offered no opportunity for the water to absorb the amounts of phosphates or calcium needed to maintain a balanced chemistry. In his research, Georges-Eugène had the benefit of his days as a law student in Paris during which, by some atavistic impulse, he chose to attend classes in hydrology at the famous Ecole des Mines.

The proprietor of the Hôtel de France reinforced Haussmann's theory. Never, he said, would he serve fish from the river that watered the Bellongue valley; the trout were of poor quality, the flesh flabby and without flavour.

The visiting doctor, not surprisingly, could not readily accept that a young bureaucrat might be right in his analysis. None the less, the two got along well. One evening, Haussmann happened to refer to someone with whom he'd been in conflict.

'He did you an injury?' the older man asked. 'In that case, he will never forgive you.'

They were words Haussmann wouldn't forget.

Water, the sustainer of life, could, then, also be life-threatening. Haussmann hardly needed a reminder of that; ten years earlier, during his assignment to Poitiers, a terrible plague of cholera descended on Paris, killing an estimated 18,000 citizens. Among them was Haussmann's mentor and minister, Casimir Perier (the same who had urged him always to praise the wives of local officials). Polluted water was suspected – and correctly so – of being the carrier. The day would come when Haussmann would declare a subterranean crusade against this dreaded killer – and would win.

He also found time to study the nearby community of St-Lizier where an establishment for treating the mentally ill was showing success with a novel approach. It consisted of separating the handicapped (among them several victims of goitre) from the insane and then putting them to work at jobs they were capable of handling. As a result, inmates who otherwise would have been doomed to rot from inactivity became useful contributors to the functioning of the institution.

For such a goal-oriented young man, St-Girons was no Nérac, with its manifold possibilities of improvement. He was in St-Girons to carry out a specific task – to end the smuggling of arms. Before long, his work produced a dramatic result. With only ten men, he and his captain captured a convoy carrying 1,000 rifles amassed by the Carlist supporters in Toulouse.

At the same time the political situation in Spain was stabilising. Judging that his work had reached a successful conclusion, Haussmann returned to Paris to discuss his next assignment. There he was shocked to learn that he was to go back to St-Girons, this time to assess the probable outcome of the next election in the *département*. He reminded the officials of their promise that he was to be rewarded with a suitable promotion. 'Please understand that your return to St-Girons is in the nature of a personal service to the minister', was the reply. Haussmann's superior, it turned out, was thinking of putting up a relative for election to the

legislature and wanted to know his chances of success. Much as he detested mixing electoral politics with his role as a public administrator, Georges-Eugène knew that his choice was clear: accept or resign. In any case, he couldn't ignore the fact that a 'personal service' to one's boss was likely to be good for one's career. He chose to accept.

He chose rightly. Finally the ministry made good its promises. Soon Haussmann was offered a choice of two posts. Neither gave him the promotion to prefect that he coveted, but both fell within the prefecture of Bordeaux where, to be close to Octavie's family, he most wanted to be stationed. With only mild regret, he accepted the job of sub-prefect of Blaye, a sleepy port on the River Gironde between the great shipping centre of Bordeaux and the Atlantic Ocean. (Forty years later he found himself stirred by nostalgia for St-Girons, even to the point of writing a highly romantic poem, largely in tribute to the beauty of the local girls – and to his own charms as a dashing young official.)

Left: None of the fountains created during the Second Empire is more imposing in itself or in its setting than the fountain of Saint-Michel across the Seine from Notre Dame Cathedral. Haussmann's mania for symmetry is seen in the two streets framing the fountain. Boulevard Saint-Michel to the east is a major artery while the deceptively noble street to the west, once penetrated, turns out to be nondescript and goes nowhere in particular.

His fourth post as sub-prefect! This, he well knew, represented too many transfers without a measurable promotion. However, the combination of Octavie's attachment to Bordeaux and his own love of the civilised life of the region, prevailed. Haussmann came to terms with the possibility that this pleasant, modest assignment might very well mark the end of his upward progress as a civil servant.

Instead, the vagaries of political life in 19th-century France turned it into a trampoline that would catapult him into the most powerful prefectorial position of the Second Empire.

PART 2

Paris, August 1854. Georges-Eugène Haussmann, prefect of the Seine, had been in office only a little more than a year when he went before the city council to propose a modernisation project even more stupefying than any of his Pharaonic programmes to date. Again, his subject that day was circulation, but this time he was speaking of the circulation of water – water coming into the city, and used water to be expelled from it.

Ordinarily Haussmann was most convincing in the role of administrator. As a public speaker, he was too factual and detailed to arouse much enthusiasm, but on this occasion his passion for his subject – health and cleanliness – seems to have inspired him. In terms of timing, his speech was dramatically linked to the news; cholera was once again creeping into the city. However, what he said was mostly designed to arouse the chauvinism of the councillors. Paris, he pointed out, was being far outdistanced by London and other cities in terms of public sanitation. How could the council take pride in creating a visually glorious new capital that was also thirsty and germ-ridden, and which tolerated the stinking pools of fetid water that accumulated in its streets?

Then came the master-stroke: 'So many habits to change and interests to convince will require the work of generations of administrators. No single prefect will be able to claim credit for such an enterprise.'

How nearly right he was can be gauged by the fact that his battle for a healthy Paris lasted almost ten years before work would even be started. The reason? The Emperor showed little enthusiasm for the subject of water. Unlike parks, boulevards and great buildings, plumbing didn't fit his concept of glory.

For the moment, Georges-Eugène cannily ruled out the possibility of honours coming his way as a result of such a long-term project. His message was clearly intended to soothe city potentates who were finding Haussmann's ascent unnerving. However, neither hindsight nor any insight into Haussmann's ambitious nature can support the idea that he was speaking with his usual directness. Can this be held against him? Hardly, in view of the nobility of his cause – which was to conquer cholera. Rather, this rare effort to appear self-effacing casts light on his complex personality. Repeatedly in his career, Georges-Eugène shoots himself in the foot with a lack of tact; he himself is his own victim. When, on the other hand, his objective is to push a worthy project to its conclusion, he is nearly always unerring. Whatever the instrument needed, he found it in his armoury. Toughness? He would crack down with his own imposing weight and the imperial power he had at his disposal. Charm? No one was a more delightful host or better able to please others (if he thought them worth the trouble!). Persuasion? His wizardry with figures repeatedly convinced the councillors that in fact financial means existed when they were certain they did not.

In the matter of water he was, in fact, talking about an obsession. Whether in his personal hygiene or in his ambitions for Paris, he was far ahead of his times. If he needed a model in the matter, he had no further to look than to his hero, Napoleon I, who also was a victim of the outlandish habit of bathing every day. Furthermore, Napoleon, too, was fully aware of the problem of supplying sufficient amounts of water to the citizens of the capital. One day he asked his prefect to name the greatest need of the populace. The answer was direct: 'Water, sire. Give them water.' Napoleon complied in part by ordering the creation of a canal, the Ourcq, but even that source fell far short of meeting the requirements of a rapidly expanding city. Also many people convinced themselves that the quality of the water was inferior to that of the River Seine, their sole source until then.

What many adjudge to be the greatest triumph of Haussmann and his chief engineer, Eugène Belgrand, today lies unwitnessed under the pavements of Paris. They knew that bringing in pure water would be meaningless without first creating an efficient system to carry away waste. Open sewers were a feature of many streets. Cries of *'gare l'eau!'* – 'Look out for water' – filled the air as householders flung their waste water into the void. (The warning was required by city ordinance to protect passers-by.) What happened after the shower hit the street was a matter of chance. In principle, rain would sooner or later sluice the mess away but often the underground sewers that did exist were unable to deal with a run-off of any consequence.

What was taking place below ground only gradually came to be understood by the authorities. Sewage from overflowing drains found its way into the soil and then into the thousands of wells, a major source of drinking-water, that dotted the city. Not everyone was unhappy with the situation. The water carriers prospered since they were paid by householders to cart water to them from the nearest fountain. There existed also, literally, merchants of death. These entrepreneurs sold the seepage from cemeteries as an especially effective tonic. One of the most profitable sources was situated in front of the church of St-Julien le Pauvre on the left bank. From the nearby churchyard the soil yielded a particularly rich cocktail that was widely appreciated.

Notwithstanding, the city council fought successfully for ten years against Haussmann's proposals and for ten years he returned to the attack. Many councillors remained unconvinced that cholera was caused by contaminated water. Above all, they declared their affection for the water from the Seine. Although rather warm in the summer, the river water was, as Haussmann's opponents pointed out, drawn some distance from the points of discharge of the city's raw sewage. Furthermore, the intakes were placed at a certain depth, supposedly assuring that floating filth would not enter the system. Finally – and perhaps the real reason behind the ardour for the Seine water – was the question of cost. It was cheap – very cheap when compared to Haussmann's scheme to pipe in fresh river water from the distant countryside.

The opposition's argument based on cost finally crumbled in the wake of the annexation of the nearby suburbs into the city of Paris. Some, such as Montmartre and Belleville, were situated on high land, requiring the construction of an enormously expensive pumping system to link them to the Seine. The plan of Haussmann and Belgrand relied on gravity, rather than steam power, by piping in fresh water from a higher elevation. Oddly, the advanced thinking of Belgrand and Haussmann hit on a conservative solution dating from the Roman Empire: the construction of aqueducts.

But the first essential was to install a sewage system capable of carrying away the waste of the old city together with that generated by the newly absorbed villages. (The French word for suburbs is '*banlieue*' – literally, 'banished place'. Today, as then, many people of modest means indeed feel banished when forced to move to the poorer suburbs.)

Belgrand's men set to work night and day under atrocious conditions. Not surprisingly, recruiting was a problem – until the rumour spread (or was spread) that lost coins and jewellery lay hidden in the muck. To harvest these riches, the recruits first had to clear away the filth accumulated over the years in the decaying tunnels. After that, it became a matter of drilling larger arteries and multiplying their number in order to produce an interlocking system of drainage. In the end, they multiplied the mileage of tunnels by five times – and did so in an incredibly short period of five years. Not only was the extent of the system vastly increased, but the size of the tunnels was dramatically enlarged. The old conduits never measured more than six feet in height whereas their replacements were as large as twelve feet high and never less than six and a half feet – sufficient to accommodate a Haussmann without stooping.

During the decade of wrangling with the municipal council, Haussmann never flagged in his determination that every Parisian residence would be served with pure water. Until he won his way, he had to content himself with other displays of water. After the Bois de Boulogne and the Bois de Vincennes, he created other lakes in his larger green spaces such as the Parcs Monceau and Montsouris and the Square du Temple.

Meanwhile, he ordered the drilling of several artesian wells whose pure water was forced to the surface by underground pressure. While most have been shut down, artesian water can today be sampled in the Square Lamartine in the 16th *Arrondissement*. A simple and handsome block of marble holds taps from which the locals daily draw their supply of spring water. Not far away in Auteuil, the Rue de la Source and the Rue de la Cure are reminders of the underground waters that were reputed to offer important health benefits.

Nor did the prefect neglect to erect fountains fed by the waters of the Seine. One of the most spectacular of these resulted from his decision to implant an important landmark at the point where the new Boulevard St-Michel meets the Seine. No neighbourhood of Paris reaches further into the past. The Romans founded the town of Lutèce there on the left bank around the year 200. Two hundred yards to the south-east are the ruins of their baths and not much farther away the remains of an arena. Across the St-Michel bridge is the island to which the city retreated in its defence against the incursions of Norman pirates. On the Ile de la Cité, Lutèce became Paris and work began on the cathedral of Notre-Dame in the 12th century.

To mark this important nexus, Haussmann commissioned a fountain for the foot of the boulevard. Another of his celebrated creative team, the architect Gabriel Davioud, designed the Fontaine de St-Michel. It measures eighty feet in

height and forty-five feet across. This huge creation presents three façades, all of equal dimension, that convey a massive nobility. On the river side, framed by four Corinthian columns, a bronze St-Michel is destroying the dragon. Beneath his feet, water spills from a semicircular basin into a shimmering pool below. The west side of the structure faces a wide street, the Rue Danton, which angles off to nowhere in particular. It is there because of the prefect's passion for order and symmetry: The east façade borders the important Boulevard St-Michel; ergo, the opposite side also must have an imposing street.

While this fountain is the largest he commissioned, Haussmann's hand is seen in other elaborate and equally impressive fountains dotted around Paris. Notable are those flanking the entrance to the Avenue de l'Opéra in the 1st *Arrondissement* and the allegories of commerce to be found in the Place des Arts et Métiers (3rd *Arrondissement.*)

For the pleasure of the public today, an introduction to the sewers of Paris has been created at the Quai d'Orsay, near the Eiffel Tower. There the visitor can see a tiny portion of the great system whose underground canals trace the network of streets above. Even the street signs of porcelain, with their typical white letters on a deep-blue background, are there to be seen. Also on display are examples of the ingenious cleaning wagons, designed by Haussmann himself, whose inspiration came from the boats used to clear the swamps around Blaye. These machines course the sewers in their interminable mission to clear the system of accumulated waste that could restrict the flow of water.

Royal visits to Paris are no longer highlighted by tours of the vast labyrinth that is the Paris sewage system. In Haussmann's time this was considered one of the most thrilling sights of all. But the ladies were advised to arrive with a phial of perfume in hand.

Belgrand, like the landscape engineer Alphand from Bordeaux, illustrates Haussmann's unerring eye for excellence in choosing his associates. In Eugène Belgrand's case, their meeting took place in Auxerre where Georges-Eugène was prefect before being summoned to Paris. In nearby Avallon, Belgrand had created an impressive fountain of artesian spring water which won the admiration of the prefect. Haussmann sampled the water and demanded to know the geology of the terrain that had produced it. He wanted to compare the underground formation with those he had researched in St-Girons. Many friendships are sealed with champagne; in this case, a cup of water sufficed. Belgrand died in 1879, twelve years before Haussmann, but not before the second great reservoir the two men planned went into operation.

Finally, with the creation of a sewage system that was winning the admiration of the world, Haussmann was in a position to realise his decade-old dream – to bring fresh, pure drinking-water into the capital. Prodigious as was his concept of a modern waste-disposal network, the prefect's idea for ending Paris's chronic water shortage dwarfed it. By means of viaducts, he envisaged reaching 100 miles out from Paris to tap the waters of the Rivers Huis and Vanne to the south. But once the flow reached the capital, what then? Reservoirs would be needed to store

Left: This machine for cleaning the sluices of the Paris sewer system owes its existence to Haussmann's experience as sub-prefect in Blaye, not far from Bordeaux. In addition to multiplying the number of paved roads throughout the county, he also ordered the drainage of unhealthy marshland, calling upon Dutch engineers for help. They introduced him to this type of apparatus which he later adapted to the needs of Paris.

the water before it was distributed throughout the capital. Once again, Haussmann's ideas were revolutionary, but, once grasped, totally rational. To store and preserve the purity of the water, he opted for lakes reaching deep underground. Here he was aided by the centuries of building and rebuilding that mark the history of Paris. Beneath the surface lay vast galleries of mined-out quarries. Some of the most extensive were in the area around Montsouris on the southern edge of the city near the Cité Universitaire. Far below the heedless thousands passing overhead, these huge spaces almost seemed to lie waiting, in their echoing, unvisited depths, to contribute once again to the well-being of the city.

In the prefect's own words, the underground galleries and sewage system function like the human body. 'Pure, fresh water circulates under the urban skin just like the fluids that support life. Secretions take place mysteriously and maintain health without troubling the orderly functioning of the city and without spoiling its external beauty.'

Ménilmontant, the first great reservoir of Paris, lies in a little visited corner of the 20th *Arrondissement* between the Rue Darcy and the Boulevard Mortier. Pedestrians see only the grass embankments that mark its perimeter. What the walls conceal is an example of the practicality and the vision of Haussmann. Here also were kilometres of abandoned quarries, deep enough to accommodate a reservoir of not just one, but two levels. Why not make use of one level to store water not fit for drinking? It could be used for street-cleaning and fire-fighting, activities for which the use of pure water would be a waste. So reasoning, he ordered Belgrand to build a great reservoir in two tiers – the upper level to store drinking-water, the lower to hold the impure water. Aside from the practicality of such an arrangement, it served politically to demonstrate to the municipal authorities Haussmann's determination to avoid waste. (Although his costs regularly overran estimates – usually because of unforeseeable complications – he showed a concern for economy. Further evidence: he insisted on auctioning off the wreckage left from the demolition of thousands of buildings.)

Work on the second huge Paris reservoir, adjacent to the Parc Montsouris, was begun in 1867 but interrupted by the Franco–Prussian War. Completed by Belgrand after Haussmann's 'resignation', it remained for decades the largest reservoir in the world, having a surface area of 456,000 square feet. Visitors are no longer admitted, but even if they were, they would be unlikely to see into the depths of the ancient quarries. There swim trout, blinded by the obscurity, who exist to verify the purity of the water. As with the canaries kept in coal-mines, the health of the fish is constantly monitored. Any sign of illness causes the vast system to be shut down while the possibility of pollution is checked out.

To distribute the water throughout the city from the reservoirs was the simplest phase of the vast project. The sewer tunnels were already in place. Threading through them the system of relatively narrow pipes needed to carry water was, in comparison, child's play. For the first time the people of Paris were able to turn a tap in their home instead of having to await the arrival of the water-carriers – with their bill for services rendered.

The entire project was an accurate reflection of Haussmann's personality and character. First of all, it required the iron will of a Haussmann to convince sceptics on all sides that the cost could only be weighed in the balance with human lives. Then, again, water and cleanliness were his weapons against the filth that so horrified him in the medieval city he felt it was his mission to sanitise. The challenge was to his measure, but he was aided by the fact that this work could be accomplished without the impediments – physical and political – that dogged his projects above ground. Below, he could give full reign to his preference for moving in a straight line from concept to fruition; what was on paper in Belgrand's projections was exactly what emerged in reality.

But the result was far more than a model of planning and execution. The reality was, above all, the total defeat of cholera in Paris. The killer of tens of thousands of Parisians no longer could find lodging in, or under the city. Another reality was that the average resident found his supply of water increased fivefold.

Could such a grandiose accomplishment, hidden as it was below ground, be compacted into a small space? Haussmann thought so. He exhibited a glass container of water from the reservoir of Ménilmontant. It was so clear in its purity that one could read through the tube the fine print of a newspaper. In any case, Belgrand was ready with scientific data testifying that the purity and mineral content of the water was beyond reproach.

But what about the cost to the consumer? Haussmann installed a system whereby the charge for water was linked to the level of rent each householder paid. There was more behind his approach than the concept of social justice. Georges-Eugène was a crusader, and among his battles was to motivate the Parisians to bathe more often and use more soap. Cheap water, he figured, would lure the great unwashed – the vast majority of the populace – in that direction. Over a period of time, he was proved right.

Although humour would seem out of place in Haussmann's concrete world of budgets, demolition, engineering and construction, he enjoyed a joke. At one state luncheon his fellows at table tried to make him look foolish by tempting him to exhibit his vanity. 'Surely', they said, 'as a result of your great accomplishments, you are well on the way to being named a count by the Emperor.'

Since the title of count was always coupled with the name of a city or town, the others went on to suggest a few localities, starting with Paris, which was impossible because of a royalty franchise. Another suggested title was 'Duc d'Huis', after the river which was soon to provide Paris with its fresh water.

'But that's not important enough for me,' said Haussmann. His interlocutor leaned forward, entranced at a chance to expose the swollen pride of the prefect.

'So what then would be satisfactory? The title of prince perhaps?'

'No, that would be too much. But I think I have the answer. I should become the *Aqua-Duc*.'

Defeated, his mockers had no choice but to force a laugh. It is said that Napoleon III also laughed, but certainly with more pleasure than those who had been so deftly put down. An amusing story, but one that illustrates Haussmann's dangerous tendency to prove himself brighter than most of his contemporaries.

Less amusing was an additional and growing threat to public hygiene. Haussmann had long been preoccupied by the overcrowding of the cemeteries. The burying grounds of the city were not only overcrowded but exuded a miasma of corruption. The seepage from decaying cadavers now threatened to overwhelm the sources of underground water that fed the city's wells and its fountains of drinking-water. Entrepreneurs discovered a growing market for a more concentrated product, rich in organic wastes. One advertised 'Sulphuretted water; cures all kinds of sickness. For only two sous a glass, you can drink this liquefied putrefaction.'

Haussmann appointed a commission to explore possible solutions. The group recommended the establishment of an immense new cemetery to the north of Paris. But once again the prefect came under fire. 'It's not enough for M. Haussmann to evict the living from their homes. Now he must exile the dead.' A woman whose son was buried in the Montmartre cemetery headed the crusade in favour of eternal rest in Paris for the Parisian dead. 'M. the prefect,' she proclaimed, 'all civilisations, even those we call barbaric, respect their dead.'

Despite his knowledge that the city would have to deal with 50,000 bodies annually in the years ahead, Haussmann could not cope with this particular tide of emotion. However, time fought the battle for him; in 1929 a huge cemetery was created just north of Paris.

Anyone could be forgiven for believing that a gigantic project such as the creation of a wholly new sewer and water distribution system would have fully occupied the prefect's time. That would not take into account Haussmann's nature. From 1865, when he won authorisation to proceed with his plan, until 1870 when Haussmann 'resigned' his post, an incredible total of eighteen new or reconstructed streets, avenues and boulevards was added to those already completed. They include such major thoroughfares as the Rue des Ecoles and the completion of the Boulevard St-Germain on the Left Bank; and, on the Right Bank, the Rue Lafayette (to link the Gare du Nord and the Gare de l'Est with the western side of the city). Notable also was the completion of an additional three sections of – the Boulevard Haussmann!

Right: Was this the world's first underground passenger railway? One of the thrills awaiting European potentates visiting Haussmann's re-created Paris was a ride on this subterranean train through some of the 600 kilometres of the newly created network of sewers. Four booted men sloshing through the muck powered the train. Women guests were advised to come armed with a phial of perfume.

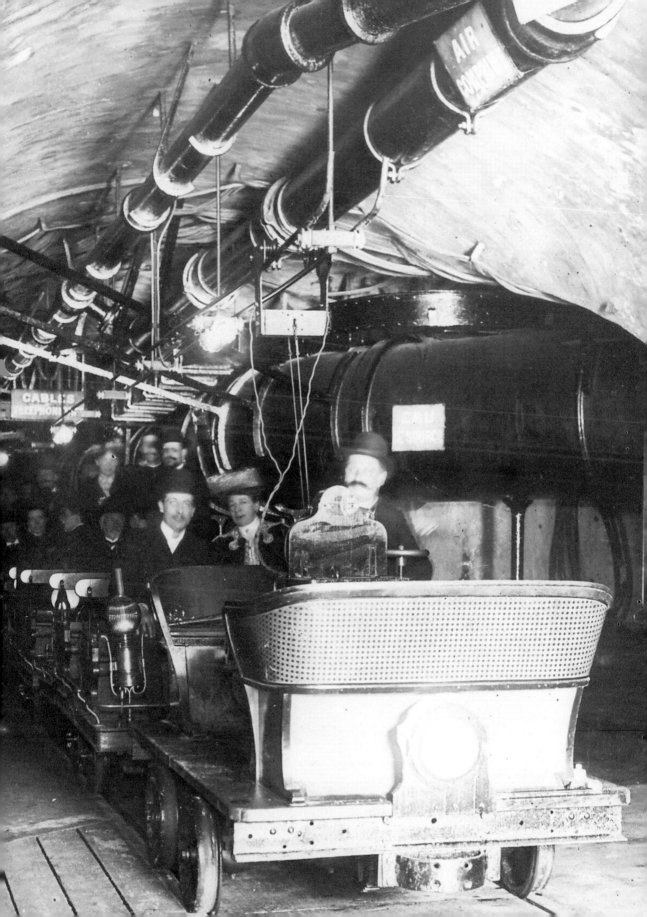

Then too there was a far less congenial demand on his time – and one that during these five years proved increasingly dangerous for him and his boss. After more than a decade of almost unquestioned imperial power, the political situation in France was becoming less stable. The Republicans in the *parlement* were finding their voice again as succeeding legislative elections showed a dwindling support for the Empire. Still, they didn't dare to attack – yet – the Emperor directly. Identifying a less dangerous victim required no particular research. They needed a target closely associated with Napoleon III, preferably one who had benefited repeatedly from his favours. Ideally that person would have made enemies through his repeated use of the imperial authority. Their prey also would have done things to stir the resentment of large segments of the populace. If such an individual could also be accused of reckless waste of the public's money – perhaps in the process, they hoped, lining his own pockets – the opposition couldn't ask more.

In every way, Prefect Haussmann filled their requirements – except for his innate honesty. Early on, he had suggested to Napoleon III that he be granted the title of baron, since his maternal grandfather, the Baron Dentzel had died without progeny. His petition was granted.

In 1857, Napoleon III named Haussmann a Senator of the Empire, a supposedly life-time appointment to a body that was created to curb any excesses by the legislature. He was even authorised to sit in on the deliberations of the Emperor's council of ministers – the most influential governmental body – whenever the subject under consideration was the affairs of the city of Paris. Then came the award by the Emperor of the highest order of the Légion d'honneur, la Grande Croix. To cap all this, foreign rulers frequently decorated Haussmann, in recognition of his achievements as well as those of his chef at the Hôtel de Ville, not to mention his wine cellar, reputed to be one of the most splendid in France. Not very wisely, the baron requested Napoleon's permission to wear his foreign decorations, contrary to custom, at state occasions. Again – and perhaps unfortunately – the Emperor went along.

The baron was a big target, in every way!

Below: Twenty-six of the most spectacular fountains in Paris were created under Haussmann's regime. To his passion for water and its hygienic qualities was added a zest for beautification, as exemplified by this fountain at the entrance to the Avenue de l'Opéra. Paris remains the only city in the world with two water supplies – pure water for personal use, river water for street-cleaning, fire-fighting and some fountains.

4
STYLE

1851. For Georges-Eugène, his assignment as sub-prefect in the sleepy port of Blaye was a kind of homecoming. Situated only 30 miles down-river from the great port of Bordeaux, the sub-prefecture encompassed 55 rural communities mostly devoted to the production of excellent wines. Haussmann's headquarters were quite different from those he had thrown together at the Hôtel de France in St-Girons. They were located in a solid tree-shaded house on the edge of town. Above the office were and are three bedrooms and at the back a pleasant walled garden. Beyond all expectations, he even found the place equipped with a bathroom! The ensemble could have made an agreeable home for the young couple and their daughter – except for Haussmann's polarisation towards Bordeaux, where his boss, the prefect, was headquartered and also where the home of Octavie's family was located. In other words, the city was for him the centre of action, both professionally and personally. In time he became something of a reverse-commuter, leaving Bordeaux Tuesday mornings and returning at noon on Saturdays.

Few commuters are blessed with more agreeable transport than the small steamer that plied the Gironde between Blaye and the elegant port city upriver. The arrangement also had its practical side. Depending on the tide, the trip lasted two to four hours during which the sub-prefect could get his paperwork done without interruption. Otherwise he soaked up useful information, chatting with the merchants and winegrowers who shared his trips. Octavie occasionally went with him, particularly when they were obliged to invite the local notables for an official reception or dinner, or were themselves guests at a nearby château. At one of these – the Château Mirambeau – the Haussmanns felt particularly at home; the Countess Duchâtel worshipped the memory of the great Napoleon to such an extent that she placed fresh flowers every day at the base of a marble bust of the Emperor. Haussmann, having had two Napoleonic grandfathers, respected a devotion which he fully shared.

Once again, he found himself an organiser of festivities, this time on behalf of the count and countess who relished playing host and hostess to visiting dignitaries. Despite the countess's preference for Napoleon, she was sufficiently broad-minded to entertain the younger son of the reigning King Louis-Philippe (and father of Haussmann's classmate, the Duc d'Orléans). Georges-Eugène remembered the company joining in a toast that went, 'On the banks of the most beautiful river in

the world, with the best of wines, let us drink to the best of kings.' After all, Napoleon had been an emperor, not a king.

But it was Bordeaux that magnetised Haussmann – above all, the handsome city itself – so far removed from the squalor of medieval Paris. Then, too, he was able to enjoy the comfort of a luxurious apartment in the home of his father-in-law, M. Laharpe, as well as a lively social life. The transplanted Swiss was well connected with people who counted, among them the Baron Sers, Haussmann's boss, prefect of the *département* of the Gironde. The baron's wine cellar was as celebrated as his table. At such dinners the future prefect of the Seine ingested directly a cabalistic knowledge of fine wines that enabled him later to create what was widely considered to be the greatest cellar in Paris.

In Bordeaux Georges-Eugène and Octavie made a pleasing picture when out strolling or shopping – he so tall and imposing, she diminutive and modest. Add their huggable blonde daughter, Henriette, and it is not surprising that the young family met with approving smiles from all. Clearly the young Haussmann family was above reproach, even among the staid bourgeois circles they frequented.

This idyllic description might give the impression that Haussmann, at the age of 32, was lapsing into a kind of pre-retirement. Nothing could be further from his nature. The very stagnation of Blaye set his hormones racing. The somnolence of the town was personified by the mayor who hated problems. His attachment to the quiet life was such that he threatened to take to his bed, ill, whenever the sub-prefect proposed to discuss any situation that might possibly turn out to be controversial. Fortunately certain members of the municipal council were not like him. With their help Haussmann was able to expand the five streets of Blaye into a network of roads linking the communities of this sub-prefecture. In a comment that forecast what lay in store for Paris, one mayor said: 'You have written your name all over the soil of our county in the form of the roads you have created.' His passion for spreading literacy resulted within two years in almost a fourfold increase in school enrolment. At the same time, using techniques borrowed from the Dutch, he set about draining the swamps adjoining the town. Such arcane knowledge always remained at the ready in his bank of information; this particular technique proved useful when he later confronted the problem of drainage that plagued Paris. Before long commerce in Blaye was stirring. During Haussmann's six years as sub-prefect, the tonnage of merchandise and agricultural products moving through the port more than doubled.

Only eight months after his arrival in Blaye, tragedy struck France and in particular Georges-Eugène. His former schoolmate and protector, the Duc d'Orléans, died instantly on 13 July 1842 in a carriage accident at the Porte Maillot in Paris where today a touching chapel to his memory stands. The immensely popular son of Louis-Philippe might have changed the course of French history had he lived to replace his ageing father on the throne. For Haussmann the death was a practical, as well as a personal blow. 'In terms of the future of my career, the passing of this affectionate mentor was an irreparable loss,' he wrote.

As events would soon prove, his statement turned out to be an exaggeration. Only six months later, he was offered the sub-prefecture of a more important centre within the prefecture of Bordeaux – the town of Libourne, a post he had earlier coveted. His surprising refusal of such a promotion owed little to a strong attachment for the inbred society of Blaye. (And Libourne was even closer, by sixteen miles, to Bordeaux.) Rather, he was determined that his next change would be to the post of full prefect – no matter where. Georges-Eugène had had enough of shunting from sub-prefecture to sub-prefecture. Moreover, his decision was linked to family stability; one year later his second daughter, Fanny-Valentine was born – like her sister – at the home of his in-laws. Because of the number of British exporters of 'claret' (Bordeaux) wines, Haussmann learned to speak English – a useful accomplishment later in Paris which may have had something to do with his choice of the name 'Fanny'.

The birth created one more link to Bordeaux. In every sense the city had become his home – far more so than dishevelled Paris ever had been. Not only was his circle of friends widening, but Bordeaux – in contrast to the Paris of his formative years – matched his idea of what a great city should be. Very likely his mind's eye superimposed on his image of Paris the elegant metropolitan setting in which he moved. Here, almost a century before, had been created parks, broad boulevards and gracious residences. If a city built by wine-growers, shippers and traders could provide air and pleasing vistas for its inhabitants, how had Paris – the home of kings – failed so miserably to do so? Inevitably, Georges-Eugène's questing mind reached out for the answer. Without surprise, he learned that the miracle of Bordeaux was attributable, not to the wisdom of politicians, but to the determination and creativity of a single-minded man – an aristocrat, Louis-Urbain Aubert, the Marquis de Tourny.

Haussmann's admiration for de Tourny's genius would later become a key element in the transformation of Paris. But for the time being, France everywhere was in a process of transformation as the railways thrust their tentacles into the countryside. A Paris world's fair in 1844 displayed the latest industrial marvels. Everyone seemed to be getting richer – the entrepreneurs, the speculators and especially those close to the centre of political power. In reality the country was rapidly sliding into depression because farming, still its major source of wealth, was suffering through two disastrous years because of bad weather. How Haussmann, situated in an agricultural region and usually so attuned to his times, could have missed – as he did – the warning signs remains a mystery.

Amidst the deceptive euphoria, Haussmann received word of his promotion to the next rank – officer – of the Légion d'honneur. Coming his way at the early age of 38, the award convinced him that his goal, a post as prefect, was almost in sight.

Georges-Eugène was right – and he was wrong. Late in 1847 he received word that he would soon be named full prefect in the not too distant city of Angoulême. Not only was his career goal within reach but he would remain within a single day's travel to Bordeaux.

The appointment never arrived. In January of 1848 the festering discontent of the people erupted into the streets of Paris. Now 72 years old, the colourless but well-meaning 'citizen king', Louis-Philippe, had no fight left. Least of all did he want to see blood shed again. Instead, he fled Paris for nearby Dreux, was there overtaken by the triumphant Republican militia and then managed to slip away to England. In one of the ironies of history, an ambitious nephew of the great Napoleon ended his exile in England and landed in France on the day the king set sail. But Louis Napoleon's moment had not yet come. Nor had that of Georges-Eugène Haussmann.

Overnight France was no longer a Monarchy. It became a Republic, confronting Haussmann, for the first time, with a fundamental choice of loyalties. This had not been the case back in 1830 when he and his family put aside their Bonapartist adherence to join the Revolutionaries who replaced the last Bourbon king, Charles X, with Louis-Philippe. After all, Georges-Eugène himself had been wounded in that fracas and decorated by the new government. Not only was the new king a well-meaning person, but Georges-Eugène's friendship with his elder son made the transition emotionally uncomplicated. Now, however, the change that came overnight was basic; nothing in Haussmann's character drew him to the idea of a Republic. To him, the Republic that had sprung 50 years earlier from the Revolution represented evidence enough of egalitarian confusion, conflict and disorder. Nor, on the other hand, was he a reactionary conservative. His ideas remained fundamentally imperialistic – in other words, he favoured a strong

Above: Before Haussmann, the area around Notre-Dame Cathedral was the centre of activity in Paris. The baron changed that, moving the focus westward to the Opéra and the St-Lazare rail terminal,

shown above with a modern sculpture in the foreground. The westward drift has continued today; more passengers, mostly commuters, pass through its gates than through those of any other Paris terminal.

central authority but one sworn to carry out the will of the people as expressed in free elections.

Clearly Haussmann could not, in good conscience, serve a government which he construed as representing the rule of the rabble. At the same time, he was thoroughly dedicated to the advancement of his career. He had known that rare satisfaction – of doing something he deemed to be supremely good while standing at the threshold of the full deployment of his talents. In practical terms, the speed of the change left Haussmann with no choice but to rely solely on his instincts rather than his connections. How he handled the situation was proof of the soundness of the former. His integrity making it impossible for him to work for the new government, he submitted his resignation. At the same time, he took all steps necessary to preserve law and order in the region for which he was responsible. In fact, keeping the peace was not difficult; Paris was far away and the conservative burghers of Bordeaux saw that, except for a few new faces, little had changed.

Did Haussmann realise at the time how fragile the new regime was? The poet Lamartine, whom Haussmann had met at the nearby Château de la Grange, now headed the government. The haste of his party to install the Republic was due to a fear that the reactionaries would move into a void. In actuality, it was confusion, not royalty, that reigned. In Bordeaux, Haussmann's friend and boss, the Baron Sers, also resigned, leaving the prefecture adrift. When a representative of the new government finally arrived to take charge of the local scene, he found himself without a corps of experienced administrators. In a humiliating decision, he asked Haussmann to stay on. However, unlike many turncoats at the time, the sub-prefect, to his credit, refused.

A further sign of the desperation of the new government followed. A job without responsibility or authority – something called the presidency of the prefectorial committee – became vacant. Wanting at least to benefit from Haussmann's good reputation, the temporary (as it turned out) government offered him the post. This time he accepted, reasoning that, without authority, he could not be accused of carrying out the will of the revolutionaries.

Below left: The doors of early Haussmannian apartment houses are immense, often to permit the entrance of horses and tall carriages.

Haussmann later wrote about his feelings: 'I left one post as a bishop and entered another as a miller.' Even so, his decision represents a fine line between principle and opportunism. In fact, both were served; without any real power, he was able to take his leave of Blaye gracefully, announcing that, as he put it, he had been 'called to other duties'. Before he did so, the loyal Octavie once again had a chance to prove her mettle. While her husband was off in Bordeaux, she was left behind to tidy up their affairs in Blaye. Once Haussmann's back was turned, the mayor of Blaye seized the occasion to name, and attempt to install, George-Eugène's successor. Octavie protested and immediately notified her spouse. He rushed back to Blaye, named his own candidate and swore him into office in an appropriately formal ceremony conducted before the mayors of his district. Haussmann was a man who insisted that affairs be handled properly – in good order – revolutions or no.

It was his last official act. Days later, his departure from the region he had dominated for six years turned out to be an emotional occasion. Virtually the entire population flocked to the pier for a farewell ceremony as he and Octavie boarded the little steamer for the last time.

Once established in Bordeaux his position was essentially that of a spectator. Although without authority, he was required to tour the entire prefecture to supervise the lottery that determined which young men would be drafted into the military. Making his rounds, he was able to learn how shallow were the roots of the republican revolution. The average person was ill-informed, and not very interested in the events taking place in Paris. Some even thought Lamartine was a woman – La Martine. Most particularly, the large and small landowners were conservative, but not radical enough to rise up against the republican revolution.

The administrative bumbling that was so evident in south-west France was increasingly damaging to the new regime in Paris where some 150,000 workers were unemployed. Seeking a solution, the government decided to send most of the job-seekers back to the provinces or to induct them into the military. Instead, many of them took to the streets and set up barricades.

Meanwhile Bordeaux was without a mayor – or '*commissaire*', the preferred title at the time. Paris solicited suggestions from Haussmann among others. He in turn consulted his father-in-law whose neutrality was assured by his Swiss citizen-

Above: To combat the monotony of repetitious façades, Haussmann enlisted two allies: wrought-iron-work of varied and intricate designs, and trees which he ordered planted by the thousands. He favoured chestnuts, shown here in early bloom in front of two typical 'post-Haussmannian' apartment houses in the Avenue Georges Mandel, 16th Arrondissement.

Above: By the start of the First World War, post-Haussmannian residential architecture had exhausted itself, verging on the rococo, as this balcony, at the entrance to the Jasmin Métro station, testifies. In the twenties, architects such as Mallet Stevens sought cleaner lines, making full use of the possibilities of reinforced concrete construction.

ship. M. Laharpe knew of a respectable burgher who actually had been a member of the governing Convention that sent Louis XVI to the guillotine. Thus his credentials as a liberal revolutionary were spotless. Indeed, fifty years later this gentleman was rather feeble and not very involved, but he relished the honour that was being thrust upon him. He was a natural to become, in fact, a puppet. And who was the puppeteer? Many people suspect that the strings were to be found in the hands of Georges-Eugène Haussmann.

The year 1848 determined Haussmann's future – and, in the process consequently, the future of Paris and the nation. Not only was the king toppled and the Second Republic ushered in, but the first elections of deputies to the national assembly were held in April. The results contained a bombshell. Without campaigning, a candidate who was a resident in England won a majority in four *départements* of France. His name was Louis Napoleon and he probably was as surprised by the result as anyone. Under the recently overthrown king, he had been sentenced, as a threat to the crown, to life imprisonment in the fortress of Ham in the north-west of France. Disguised as a bricklayer, he had escaped in 1846.

Louis Napoleon ventured back on French soil, certain now that he was needed there. He received a chilly welcome from the new provisional government. Not daring to go so far as to arrest him, the regime 'suggested' that his presence in the country was unwelcome. In one of the master-strokes that Louis Napoleon repeatedly proved himself capable of delivering, he quietly withdrew to fortress England to await further developments. Ultimately, they would bring him face to face, in

Left: Haussmann's buildings are highly prized in today's Paris where there is even a 'neo-Haussmannian' revival underway. To the right, adjoining a late-Haussmann building is an example. Oddly, its modern, cost-efficient construction harks back more in its simpliity to the early Haussmannian structures than to their more ornate successors.

the newly reoccupied Elysée Palace, with a man who fully understood the magic of the name Napoleon – Georges-Eugène Haussmann.

He hadn't long to wait. The 'June Days', as they came to be called, were days written in the blood of Parisians. In placid Bordeaux, so far from the scene, the rioters were considered to be mad; there was even some talk of creating an expeditionary force that would march north to bring the capital to its senses. From his retreat in England, Louis-Philippe commented acidly: 'The Republicans are lucky. They have the privilege of shooting down their fellow citizens.'

Calm returned with the announcement that presidential elections would be held in December. Once again Louis Napoleon demonstrated that he had learned much about the value of diplomacy since the headstrong days of his youth. The

Right: *Street fairs of all kinds were a feature of old Paris. This shows the Ham Fair on the Avenue Richard Lenoir bordering the Canal St Martin.*

lessons may have been absorbed in the course of his reflections and reading at the 'University of Ham', as he called his fortress prison. He sent a message to the national assembly, simply stating 'If the people call on me to accept responsibilities, I shall know how to discharge them.'

The people called on him – overwhelmingly!

His election in the Bordeaux region was an especially spectacular victory, Louis Napoleon receiving five times as many votes as his nearest rival. Poor 'La Martine', the actual incumbent, found himself with only 537 supporters.

The chemistry of history was at work. Louis Napoleon's success in Bordeaux was, as he surely learned, more than a little due to quiet campaigning on the part of Haussmann. In turn, Haussmann's enthusiasm, never kindled by the republicans, was, as always, ignited by the name Napoleon. Soon the two men would discover their mutual passion for grandiose projects carried out with order and discipline.

Even before the historic election, letters praising Haussmann's abilities were reaching Paris. Barely a month went by after Louis Napoleon took office before Georges-Eugène was summoned to the capital by the Minister of the Interior. Their meeting went well and within hours the former sub-prefect of Blaye stood before the future Emperor of France. The scene gave no hint of the importance of their exchange. Their meeting took place in the sadly deteriorated Elysée Palace where Napoleon I had signed his abdication in 1815. The vast, draughty rooms were poorly heated and the new president of France was suffering from a cold. Louis Napoleon had moved in immediately on his election, wanting no delay in establishing any and all links with his illustrious uncle. He was fully aware that the name Napoleon – 'Polon' to the people – had counted more in his election victory than any demonstrated merits of his own.

Below: View of Notre-Dame Cathedral, obscured prior to Haussmann's arrival, by the hospital, Hôtel-Dieu. Haussmann ordered it destroyed and then rebuilt elsewhere to reveal the full splendour of the cathedral façade.

Below right: The displacement of the Hôtel-Dieu enabled the public to view the façade of Notre-Dame Cathedral from some distance. This expensive renewal project typifies Haussmann's insistence that the great Parisian landmarks from the past be given noble settings. (The building to the left is the headquarters of the Paris police.)

On this evening, those merits were hardly evident. Like his uncle, he was short, barely reaching five feet seven inches. He wore a vaguely funny moustache, pointed at the ends, and he walked with a strange cowboy-like gait. Reddened from his cold, his large nose stood out against a pasty complexion. How different from the strapping Haussmann, who seldom seems to have had a day of illness. Six inches taller than his future boss, Haussmann and the president were always more comfortable when they were seated. Despite his handicaps, Louis Napoleon possessed more than just a name. He had poise and intelligence and he knew how to charm – men as well as women. He promptly congratulated his visitor on his demonstrated ability to keep order and thanked him for his support in the presidential election. The two men were within a year of the same age and soon discovered that they shared a partiality for logic and direct communication. Nothing was concluded that evening, but Haussmann left the Elysée confident that his goal, to have his own prefecture, was within sight.

He was right. At their next meeting the president announced his decision. Haussmann was to fill a vacancy as prefect of the *Département* of the Var in Provence. It is a measure of the mutual confidence growing between the two men that Haussmann dared to signal that he was not entirely pleased. 'The Var', he observed, 'is about as far from Bordeaux as it is possible to go while still remaining in France.' Instead of showing resentment, Louis Napoleon explained that subversive elements in the department represented a threat to France's relations with Italy, just across the border. Order must be restored without delay.

Haussmann discharged his mission in fifteen months, displaying considerable physical courage as he personally faced down a mob with only feeble armed support at his disposal. This action, plus other demonstrations of firmness, made it clear that the government was now fully in charge. Then came a short period as prefect in Auxerre, on the threshold of Burgundy. This time the trouble to be dealt with was a threatened victory of the Left in a very special plebiscite. The question to be decided: whether or not Louis Napoleon's four-year tenure as president should be extended. Handicapped by a ruling that the prefects were forbidden to interfere in elections, Haussmann was nevertheless able to restore order and, largely as a consequence, to win renewed popularity for the president.

In June 1851, Louis Napoleon travelled to Auxerre where he received a gratifying ovation from the crowd. At his departure, he spoke words that would

Below: The cattle market built at the northern edge of Paris to eliminate the passage through the city streets of herds of cattle. At the time the roof surface was the largest in Europe. Today the building is an adjunct of the City of Musique at the Port of La Villette.

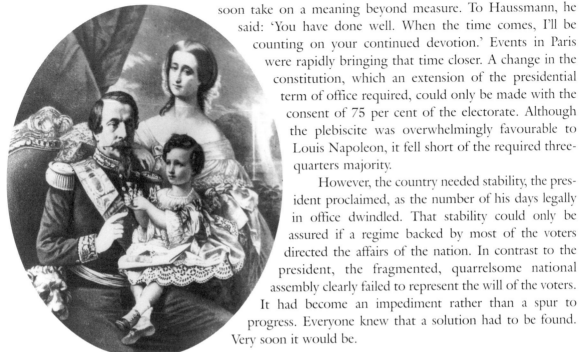

soon take on a meaning beyond measure. To Haussmann, he said: 'You have done well. When the time comes, I'll be counting on your continued devotion.' Events in Paris were rapidly bringing that time closer. A change in the constitution, which an extension of the presidential term of office required, could only be made with the consent of 75 per cent of the electorate. Although the plebiscite was overwhelmingly favourable to Louis Napoleon, it fell short of the required three-quarters majority.

However, the country needed stability, the president proclaimed, as the number of his days legally in office dwindled. That stability could only be assured if a regime backed by most of the voters directed the affairs of the nation. In contrast to the president, the fragmented, quarrelsome national assembly clearly failed to represent the will of the voters. It had become an impediment rather than a spur to progress. Everyone knew that a solution had to be found. Very soon it would be.

Above: An obviously idealised portrait of the imperial family : Napoleon III, the Empress Eugénie and their son, who died at the age of 21 fighting alongside the British army in Africa.

No greater evidence of the symbiosis between the two men exists than the fact that Haussmann became prefect of the Bordeaux region on the very same day that President Louis Napoleon staged his *coup d'état*.

The day before, 1 December, Haussmann was summoned to Paris. To his astonishment, the president announced that Georges-Eugène was to travel the next day to Bordeaux where he would assume the post of prefect – the job he had wanted above all others. But there was something strange about the sudden appointment. The president instructed Haussmann to report early – 'very early', he stressed – next morning to receive his written orders from 'the Minister of the Interior'. This was normal procedure since he was the one who directed the prefectorial service. What was decidedly abnormal, however, was the behaviour of the Minister, M. Thorigny. After dinner that evening, Haussmann said to him: 'I will look forward to being in your office early tomorrow to receive my orders.' 'Orders?' the Minister responded, 'but I have no orders for you, Monsieur.' Aware that, in some fashion, he had committed a *faux pas*, Georges-Eugène made his exit without delay. Clearly he had said the wrong thing.

At five o'clock next morning he told the receptionist at the ministry that he was there to see the minister. This elicited an astonishing question: 'M. Thorigny or M. le Comte de Morny?' At once the visitor understood; the Comte de Morny was the half-brother of Louis Napoleon. Overnight there had been a change in command. 'Announce my presence to the Comte,' Haussmann replied without hesitation.

'So you are with us,' was de Morny's greeting. Haussmann replied that he was at the service of the president, no matter what might be asked of him. That

evening, armed with orders giving him sweeping powers, he boarded a train for Bordeaux, arriving there just before dawn. It was a special dawn in French history – one that saw the constitution overturned in order to permit a second Napoleon to remain in power.

Haussmann was mistaken if he expected that his reputation among the privileged of Bordeaux would assure him a cordial welcome. Quite the reverse; M. Neveux, the incumbent, had earned a certain popularity. More significantly, he had won important support among the conservative voters who still yearned for the days of King Louis-Philippe, ousted from office four years earlier by the Republicans.

As day broke, Haussmann strode into the office of the prefect. Stacks of posters protesting the *coup d'état* lay everywhere, still warm from the printer and ready to be displayed throughout the region. The prefect, Neveux, was even preparing to deploy the powers that authorised him to call out the national guard if order were threatened. Haussmann had never hesitated to use muscle in the past and this occasion was no exception. He threw his mandate from Paris on the table, ordered the former prefect to quit the premises and the posters to be destroyed. By daybreak the new prefect of the Bordeaux region was climbing into bed at the

Below: The Place du Châtelet, showing (to the left) the Théâtre du Châtelet, one of two great theatres that preceded the building of the Paris Opéra. In the centre is the Column of Victory which Haussmann ordered, in the interest of symmetry, to be transplanted from the right side of the square.

home of his in-laws. Complying with his orders, new posters were streaming off the presses as he slept.

The drama was over almost before it had begun, but the hard work was only just beginning. There was opposition to be quelled, not because of a serious threat of violence but because a few dedicated liberals had already been at work, determined to stir up opposition to Louis Napoleon. Then came the second, more protracted, phase; the building up of support for President Louis Napoleon in the wake of his seizure of government.

Right: Crowds gathered to watch the prodigious feat of moving the vast column from the west side to the centre of the Place du Châtelet.

During these months the prefect was completing his twelfth year in and around Bordeaux, the city where he had met his wife and where his two children were born. His love of the place rivalled his abhorrence of Paris. The orderly elegance of Bordeaux stirred him and he was fascinated by de Tourny's successful city planning. Only the sixth city of France in terms of population, it was certainly the most beautiful. Here was a place where traffic and people circulated with ease in an environment pleasing to the eye. Great monuments were linked by broad streets and boulevards. Green spaces abounded, even in the centre of the city. Handsome houses of similar height and classical inspiration lined the boulevards and avenues. They could have proved monotonous except for the variations in detail provided by iron balconies and roof-top balustrades, by sculptured decoration and by small points of architectural detail. Above all, the city had a focal point – the magnificently sober theatre of the architect Victor Louis, completed in 1780, around which urban life swirled. Seen from the river, Bordeaux could be a stage setting with its rows of handsome houses extending southward from the stunning 17th-century Place de La Bourse, designed by Gabriel.

Below: The construction of the Paris opera house, popularly known today as the Palais Garnier (after its architect), as it neared completion.

This was a city that seemed built for pageantry of the kind the prefect had a gift for creating. In October 1852 he received word that he would have an opportunity to display his talents as an impresario. The president, he was advised, was planning a tour of south-western France. Haussmann must have sensed that Louis Napoleon's trip was more than simply a tour of the countryside. He wasn't taking a protracted leave of Paris for his pleasure, but rather to judge the degree of support he possessed outside the volatile capital city. But for what purpose? The answer would be not long in coming, and it would determine the history of Europe up to today – and beyond.

Even by then Haussmann understood his boss as few others did. He virtually took charge of the expedition, reversing the planning from beginning to end. He persuaded Paris to change its idea that the visit would start with Bordeaux, insisting that instead it should end there. That way, the president would come into the city by boat rather than by rail, thus starting his visit with a spectacular view of the waterfront. And ending it with memories of Bordeaux – and Haussmann's showmanship.

Everything went as Haussmann had recommended. The official vessel entered the city flanked on each side by three rows of ships lined up bow to stern. Cannon saluted, fireworks blazed and every church-bell in Bordeaux pealed. The mayor greeted the visitor at the 18th-century Hôtel de Ville, accompanied by dignitaries from every community of the prefecture. The visit went on like that for four days. The president, an excellent horseman, led a parade through de Tourny's handsome streets, thronged by most of the populace of the city. A commemorative medal was struck for the occasion and a huge, colourful banner, decorated with the arms and emblems of the Bonaparte family, floated over the entrance to the quays. Two elaborate banquets were held, the second of them the night before Louis Napoleon's departure. In the course of his speech on that occasion two sentences told the prefect what was in store. 'Empire is the way to peace,' was one of them, and, later, 'When France is satisfied, Europe is calm,' was the other. Napoleonic law and order were to reign, for the second time, in an imperial France.

This was the culmination of a momentous visit. Before and during it, Haussmann had produced something akin to a miracle. He had confronted a public formerly loyal to the departed King Louis-Philippe and infused it with a spontaneous enthusiasm for Louis Napoleon. This kind of support was what the president had been seeking during his trip. Only with it could he risk even hinting at his intentions.

But there were other words that Haussmann remembered just as vividly. They had been spoken by Louis Napoleon on his arrival, as the two stood on the deck of the boat that brought them within view of Bordeaux. Clasping the prefect's arm, the president suddenly exclaimed, 'What a magnificent city!'

Just as the visit forecast the arrival of the Second Empire so, too, did it foreshadow the future shape of the city of Paris. In 1852 the government submitted to the voters a proposal to end the Second Republic. In its stead France would again become an empire, with the president recast as emperor, the Emperor Napoleon III. Once again the vote in Haussmann's prefecture was massively 'yes'.

Left: Haussmann, studying a map of Paris surrounded by some of his achievements. Clockwise from top left: church of the Trinity, church of Saint Augustin, Place du Châtelet, Tribunal de Commerce.

Above: The buildings that encircle the Arc de Triomphe differ markedly from the 'standard' Haussmann residences, especially in height. The ground floor is partly below street level. Above there are only three storeys, plus the rooftop dormer windows. The shrinkage and the restrained use of ornamentation enhance the monumental arch, renouncing any competition with it.

This second important victory in Haussmann territory did not go unnoticed by the occupant of the Elysée Palace. In June 1853, Georges-Eugène Haussmann received a dispatch from Paris naming him prefect of the Seine. Not long before, he had turned down an offer to become both Mayor and prefect of Lyon, a position of ultimate power in the nation's third largest agglomeration. His reasons were not only personal but rooted in job satisfaction. He had exciting plans for expanding and remodelling parts of his beloved city.

To work alongside a Napoleon in transfiguring decrepit Paris was a magnet that left no room for doubt as to his response.

But would this young (44-years-old) prefect, who had worked only as a bureaucrat in the provinces, measure up to such an important job? Would he be able to survive in the arena of Paris politics or was he simply being thrown to the lions? Listen to the opinion of the Duc de Persigny, one of Napoleon III's longest-serving and most trusted aides:

'I found facing me one of the most extraordinary types of our generation. Tall, strong, vigorous, energetic, but at the same time sensitive, clever, creative and resourceful, this audacious man never hesitated to tell me openly who he was. With a certain pride, he recited the peaks of his career. He could have talked for six hours on his favourite subject – himself. I was not at all put out by this. It

exposed all kinds of facets of his strange personality. Pride in his triumphs was written on his face. As this absorbing person laid out the facts about himself with a kind of brutal cynicism, I could hardly contain my satisfaction.

'"To battle", I told myself, "against the frozen ideas and prejudices of an entire school of economic thinking, against men who were shrewd, sceptical products of the legal and financial worlds – seldom overly scrupulous in their conduct – here was the man ...." I enjoyed the idea of throwing this huge feline animal amidst the foxes and wolves arraigned against all the generous aspirations of the Empire.'

A marvellously accurate description of Haussmann! But also of the denizens of the political jungle he was about to penetrate.

PART 2

The year 1865 proved to be the apogee of everything for which Georges-Eugène Haussmann had striven for 35 years. This was certainly true in terms of his quest for power and prestige; he was now a senator, a favourite of the Emperor's and a baron of the Empire. He wore the highest order of the Légion d'honneur, and the mighty of the world could not visit Paris without being received at the Hôtel de Ville by the prefect and his wife.

True, he had not succeeded in winning the ultimate recognition which he thought, not unreasonably, was his due – to carry the title 'prefect of Paris'. On the other hand, he had won his battle – after ten long years and (for once) with only token support from the Emperor – to launch his colossal project to bring pure water into Paris.

Yet whatever the manifestations of his success, they were only that, the outward evidence of something far more important; Haussmann's real success lay in his accomplishments and he knew it. Vain though he was, power for him was, above all, a means to achieve concrete results. He was essentially a planner and builder on a scale that defies imagination. Above all, he was perhaps the first person of the millennium to conceive of a city in its entirety – not only the layout of its streets and the architecture of its buildings, but also its parks, its fountains and sanitation system and even its network of food distribution through public markets, large and small. All was accomplished with pick-and-shovel long before the advent of the trip-hammer and today's techniques of destruction by implosion. He and the American architect, Frank Lloyd Wright, would have understood each other. Whereas critics try to tar Haussmann as boastful and arrogant, Wright said of himself that he preferred 'honest arrogance to mock humility'.

Twelve years after he became prefect of the Seine, Haussmann's authoritarian style had mostly attracted carping and sniping along with some rumblings of the verbal artillery that were being rolled into place in the *parlement*. Although major demolition and reconstruction was still under way, the look of the imperial capital was now taking shape. The future could be seen and Napoleon III was able to show off with pride its emerging transfiguration. Foreign dignitaries came and marvelled – a far cry from the visit only ten years earlier when the first royal guest, Queen Victoria of England, had to be routed around the devastation to spare her from seeing the ugly scars on all sides. She began her carriage-ride through Paris from a platform specially built for her arrival adjacent to the Gare de L'Est and completed it in a procession along a still unfinished avenue leading directly to the Hôtel de Ville. There the delegation that awaited her was headed by prefect Haussmann and his wife (who so impressed the Queen that Her Majesty presented her, at the end of the visit, with a handsome broach). That early example of a truly Haussmannian avenue was – and still is – called, not surprisingly, the Avenue Victoria, though at the time many of the façades were not of dressed stone, but were painted on great sheets of canvas.

How can we account for the state of decrepitude in which one of the world's major cities had found itself? An important factor was the transfer of the court

Below: Les Halles, the central market of Paris, was housed in these buildings designed by the architect Baltard after his first construction was spurned by Napoleon III and had to be razed. Haussmann successfully mediated between a dissatisfied Emperor and a demoralised architect to produce this result, shown here as the work neared an end. Many Parisians mourned when Baltard's pioneering work, fusing glass and iron, was destroyed in 1969.

Below: The Place Saint-Germain d'Auxerrois, today the Place du Louvre, before Haussmann arrived. He demolished the buildings in the foreground but spared the church whose bells signalled the start of the Saint Bartholomew's Day massacre of Protestants in 1572. A Protestant himself, Haussmann feared that levelling the church would be seen as an act of retribution.

of Louis XIV to Versailles in the 17th century. Until then, the city had been the home of royalty. Abruptly Paris found itself disinherited, billions of francs that might have been devoted to its renewal going instead into the vast palace the Sun King erected as testimony to his own glory and that of France. Meanwhile, the population of Paris was exploding. By Haussmann's time, the city was housing – frequently in shacks and shanties – three times as many people (1,600,000 – not much fewer than today's populace) as lived there under the reign of Louis XIV. The majority of the 'medieval' buildings were not medieval at all, having been erected in the 17th and 18th centuries. Regardless of historical accuracy, their destruction was and is, in some circles today, mourned by people living in a comfort far removed from the reality of the mid-19th century. Haussmann spared many of the more solid buildings; indeed, whole neighbourhoods of old Paris still delight those who stray from the boulevards. The Marais, Ile de la Cité, Montagne Ste-Geneviève and the streets around the Rue du Sentier are only some of the reminders.

Two-thirds of the way through Haussmann's tenure, typical neighbourhoods emerged that were to become identified throughout the world as being Parisian. But Parisians themselves later came to identify that 'look' as Haussmannian.

What does Haussmannian mean? It speaks of broad, tree-lined boulevards and important avenues which are, depending on their width, lined with a single or a double row of trees. Nearly all of them are as straight as an arrow, usually beginning and/or ending with a noble monument or fountain. Pavements of vast width testify to Haussmann's disgust with the medieval streets that forced strollers to walk single-file, hugging the walls, in an effort to skirt the filth.

But what of the buildings that define the vertical geometry of the streets? Nearly all Haussmannian buildings fronting on his thoroughfares were originally intended to be places where people lived. (Today many have been converted to chic offices, everything behind the façade having been gutted and rebuilt.) The ground floor, more often than not, is occupied by stores and boutiques serving their neighbourhood. The floor immediately above these enterprises is usually occupied by the proprietor and his or her family. Activities that are artisanal in nature or devoted to light fabrication were relegated to the courtyards and unredeemed alleys behind the handsome buildings fronting on an avenue.

The façades themselves are written in blocks of dressed stone quarried from beneath the city itself. Replacing the painted cement walls of most pre-Haussmann dwellings, the stone forms a softer skin than the granite frequently found in more monumental buildings. Yet it rivals granite in durability. When clean, this

Right: Street lamps such as these are typical of Haussmann's detailed concern to beautify the city. The designs vary to harmonise with the adjacent environment.

Below: Not only did Haussmann preserve the church, but he constructed next to it the new borough hall below, of the 1st Arrondissement. So similar are the buildings that one has to look carefully to distinguish between them.

pierre de taille radiates cheerful hints of a soft lemon-like hue. On the other hand, the same stone in grey weather tends to absorb all reflection. This caprice of lighting may be why Paris can be such a cheerful city under clear skies, but rather morose when the sun is in hiding. Some people find this a key to the mood swings so often displayed by Parisians.

At first the new thoroughfares that replaced the meandering streets and alleys struck the inhabitants of the city as unbearably white and barren. The trees planted at that time were mere saplings and the weather had not yet done its job of mellowing the stone. No wonder the change dismayed many people, including the painter Pissarro whose famous *Place de l'Europe* shows a few rather glum pedestrians braving the rain in a cold and uninviting setting.

Haussmannian buildings, like most architecture, reflect their times. The 'hôtels' (the circumflex replaces an 's') of the previous century were intended to shelter family and relatives or familiars. Superb examples still exist. Among them are the Hôtel Soubise (now the National Archives) in the Rue des Francs Bourgeois, the nearby Hôtels Sevigné (now the museum of the City of Paris) and de Rohan – these and others in the Marais district of the 3rd and 4th *Arrondissements*. The Ile St-Louis, to which the aristocrats fled whenever the demands of the court of Versailles became unbearable, contains two magnificent examples: the Hôtels Lambert and de Lauzon. Perhaps the most visited of all the hôtels of Paris are the 16th-century red-brick town houses that line the celebrated Place des Vosges, built by King Henri IV just off the Place de la Bastille.

Essential to the Haussmannian style was the arrival a few years earlier of the apartment house. The word says it; no longer were the living quarters of different families intermingled in the same building. Instead, they lived totally 'apart' – one or more to a floor of 'flats', as the British neatly labelled them. The apart-ment house made it possible, even common, for families on the same floor to have no knowledge – not even perhaps the name – of the tenant across the hall.

At the same time, the correspondingly anonymous pursuits of engineering and industry were replacing the local artisans. The wealth engendered by these new gods of capitalism accounted for much of the growth of the middle and upper-middle class for whom Haussmann's buildings were designed. Possessed of no fortune himself, Georges-Eugène Haussmann's background nevertheless enabled him to perceive their needs and taste – or, as some critics claimed, lack of it. Moreover, in tune with his times, his frame of mind was essentially that of an engineer – a fact that helps explain the manner in which his buildings anticipated the art nouveau style of the twenties and the 'filing-cabinet' buildings that were strewn about the city after the Great War. Ahead of his time, Haussmann simplified design while introducing variation of detail to avoid too much monotony. It is interesting to note that Le Corbusier approved of Haussmann's work, going so far as to say: 'I am the Haussmann of today.'

In this light, it is hardly surprising that the residential buildings of the Second Empire owe more to engineering than to the Beaux-Arts architects. Or that the stonework became a little more than a curtain for structural steel frames rather than an integral part of the structure. Bridges and the superb, but now sadly lost, 'umbrellas' of ironwork that sheltered the central market-place of Les Halles, are examples of France's passion for the new materials. Before long, the greatest example of all, the Eiffel Tower, would be reaching for the skies of Paris.

Nevertheless, Paris still is, by and large, a horizontal city, a fact which Haussmannian buildings emphasise. Invariably, balconies edged with intricate iron-work highlight the second and fifth storeys (considered the two most desirable floors – the one for its easy access by stairway, the other for its light and air and spacious balcony well above the clatter of horseshoes below.) Each floor of each building corresponds to the height of its next-door neighbour. In comments as repetitive as the architecture, critics found the sameness of the buildings boring. They overlooked the variety of lacy patterns traced in iron and its shadows against pale stone. Further relief from monotony is provided by restrained variations in stonework and in the setbacks above the fifth floor. By law, no balcony, or any other element of construction, was permitted to protrude beyond clearly defined

Above: Most Paris news-stands today are of uniform design, constructed of metal and glass. With the rehabilitation of the Champs Elysées in 1997, not only was parking prohibited on the avenue, but the Haussmanian 'kiosks', like the one above, were resurrected in their original form.

Above: The Paris
flower market as it
looks today.

limits. Above all, 'respect for one's neighbour' was a fundamental concept –
discarded, unhappily, by post-Second World War builders (whose not so golden
rule seems to be 'argue with your neighbour').

Exempted from the rigid rules governing Haussmann residential architecture
are the houses ringing the Arc de Triomphe. They are four floors high instead of
five – a way to emphasise the awesome monumentality of the arch.

Haussmann animated a group that included the great architects of the
period. Mostly active in the design of public buildings, they produced some of
the great landmarks of the city. The team included Hittorff, Davioud, Baltard
and the ever-loyal Alphand for public spaces. More anonymous architects
produced such massive, unimaginative structures as the prefecture de Police on
the Ile de la Cité adjacent to another equally depressing building, the new
Hôtel Dieu. The location of the hospital uncomfortably close to Notre-Dame
Cathedral triggered still more invective. While the attackers drew a bead on
Haussmann for even rebuilding the Hôtel Dieu, they had the wrong target. In
fact, Napoleon III opposed Haussmann's desire to relocate the hospital,
insisting that he would not tolerate depriving the residents of the centre of the
city of medical services while erecting a palace devoted to the pleasures of rich

opera-goers. He ignored one fact: under Haussmann, the 'centre' was shifting to the north and west.

Charles Garnier, the architect of the Opéra, was not a member of the prefect's architectural team; his design had been chosen in a competition sponsored by the city. When the Empress Eugénie inspected Garnier's plans for the building, she was bewildered. 'But this doesn't correspond to any school of architecture,' she, in effect, complained. Garnier bowed and replied: 'But, Madame, my theatre does represent an important new style – that of Napoleon III.'

The story is more amusing than accurate. There is, in fact, no 'Napoleon III' architecture; there is only a Haussmannian no-nonsense cityscape. As magnificent as the new opera house turned out to be, its meaning for Haussmann was important in an even larger context. He saw it as a vital focal point marking the new centre of the city. The concept clearly harks back to the prefect's attachment to Bordeaux and the key place the 'Grand Théâtre' held in de Tourny's city planning.

Below: Victor Hugo and others were upset by the demolition of most of the dwellings around Notre-Dame Cathedral. However, many of them were doomed to collapse under their own weight, as this view of the Rue du Marché-aux-fleurs (Flower-Market Street) testifies. This is one of the many scenes in this book attributable to Charles Marville, the photographic genius engaged by Haussmann to record the transformation of Paris.

Below: One of the old streets destroyed to make way for the Tribunal de Commerce.

By choosing the site of the Opéra, Haussmann recognised – and abetted – the drift
of the city away from Notre-Dame towards the western districts.

Other theatres were built with no reference to the style of Garnier's palace. Two
of the most prominent face each other across the Place du Châtelet. Designed
by Davioud, they use glass lavishly in the design of the façades – as in New
York's Lincoln Center – framed within stonework that is vaguely Italian. The
larger of the theatres, the Théâtre du Châtelet, with its 2,200 seats, was the
largest theatre in Paris before the completion of the 'Palace Garnier'. The two
speak more of Haussmann's uncluttered mind than of Garnier's flamboyance. In
fact, the square in its entirety bears Haussmann's stamp, particularly his mania
for order and equilibrium. The creation of the Boulevard de Sébastopol, an
artery absolutely essential to the north-south axis of the new Paris, inconve-
niently entered the east side of the Place du Châtelet. This meant that an
immense column topped by a golden statue of victory, with at its base a fountain watered by four huge sphinxes, was no longer situated in the centre of the
Place. Notwithstanding the fact that the huge ensemble rose 66 feet above the
ground and weighed hundreds of tons, the prefect ordered it to be moved. On
21 April 1858, Parisians flocked to watch, unbelievingly, this prodigious operation bossed by Davioud himself, which placed the column where it now is – in
the exact centre of the square.

Then came yet another complication; if centred atop Hittorff's new Tribunal
de Commerce, as would be normal, the cupola that crowned the building could

not be seen from the new Boulevard de Sébastopol. Never daunted where a noble perspective was involved, Haussmann simply ordered the dome to be moved to the edge of the roof facing the Boulevard du Palais.

This was hardly an elegant solution, but when forced to choose between his love of a noble vista and architectural logic, Haussmann sacrificed logic. Leaving one of the many cafés bordering the Place du Châtelet, a diner might wonder if the wine was responsible for the displaced dome.

A 'Napoleon III' architecture? The Châtelet speaks clearly: what was being created was a 'Haussmannian' style: geometrical, orderly (except for that dome) and without clutter. At each intersection the corners of his buildings were either snipped off or rounded, again with a practical purpose. The amputations enabled coachmen to see traffic about to enter from left or right, which might have reduced the number of collisions. (The prefect also ordered all vehicles to steer to the right instead of the left as another safety measure.)

Although their thinking was very different, there is no evidence that Garnier and Haussmann were at loggerheads. Garnier, however, was hardly generous in his opinion of the prefect's work: 'Uniformly constructed, uniformly aligned, with only rare exceptions, the buildings of this period tend to lose any pretence at personal individuality.'

Because he was so in tune with his times, Haussmann's basic concepts long survived his lifetime. 'Individuality' crept in after 1882 when building regulations

Above: The Tribunal de Commerce across the Seine from the Place du Châtelet. To be certain that the dome was perfectly in the line of sight from the new Boulevard Sébastopol, Haussmann ordered the dome to be placed off-centre, as shown here.

were relaxed, enabling the newly rich bourgeoisie to flaunt their self-importance. One of the more restrained early modifications that crept into Haussmannian façades was a proliferation of ironwork. Near the turn of the century, bosomy goddesses, muscular weight-bearers and flourishing floral patterns added to the pomp that the bourgeoisie demanded. However, as late as 1893 'pure' Haussmannian structures were still being built – for example, at 147 Avenue Mozart in the 16th *Arrondissement*. In juxtaposition, just across the avenue, at 122, stands an apartment building designed in 1910 by Guimard (famous for the ironwork *Métro* entrances that still dot the Paris scene). Its decorative exterior heralded the advent of Art Nouveau and foreshadowed the end of the post-Haussmann period.

In 1867, a new invention made its appearance and changed the class stratification inside the buildings. The elevator, originally driven hydraulically, was redefining the concept of luxury. The fifth floor with its large balcony, panoramic views and relatively pure air replaced the second (known as the 'noble' floor) as the preferred place to live.

Below: The final section of the Louvre Palace under construction in 1855 during the reign of Napoleon III and the supervision of Haussmann.

In contrast to housing, the public buildings created by Haussmann's architects are the products of his associates who were given the liberty of creating splendid displays of virtuosity. They are typified by six new mini Hôtel de Ville from which the *arrondissements* of Paris, each with its own mayor, are administered. Such buildings are intended to impress the public with the power of the authorities – and they succeed admirably in their role.

In 1867, Haussmann won still another honour. Elected to the august Académie des Beaux-Arts, he confided, revealingly, that he would have

preferred to have been inducted into the Académie des Sciences. Perhaps he had in mind the most revolutionary of all the edifices being constructed under his supervision – the railway terminals – the Gare du Nord and the Gare St-Lazare in particular.

Today it is impossible to feel the shock-waves that Haussmann's private architecture sent through all segments of Paris society. The so-called working class had the most cause for complaint. Not only were rents soaring out of reach, but the apartments behind the stone façades invariably boasted unneeded (for them) servants' quarters and elegant rooms overlooking the new thoroughfares. The 'double reception' was a fixture of even the smaller apartments. Tenants were expected to receive guests – sometimes in limited numbers, requiring the use of only one reception room. For larger parties, sliding glass doors could be thrown open to double the space available.

Above: Would Haussmann approve of the glass pyramid in the middle of the courtyard of the Louvre? More an engineer than an architect, and not

Servants were often numerous. They were housed in the attic of a typical Haussmann building, in cramped rooms, sweltering in summer, bone-chilling in winter, lighted by small dormer windows, and limited in terms of sanitary facilities. The help was expected to use a steep staircase at the back of the building. The lifestyle of the tenants is well illustrated by the fact that the kitchen was often located at the rear end of the apartment to avoid cooking smells in the dining room at the other end. The obvious inefficiency of this arrangement was not troublesome – if one had servants to hustle the food to the table while still hot.

However, Haussmannian residential buildings offered an astonishing variety of accommodation, created by a simple process of addition and subtraction. A reception-room eliminated, bedrooms reduced in number and servants' quarters curtailed ... thus even the 'less rich' could find lodgings in certain of the new build-

ings. But not the ordinary citizens displaced by the demolitions. They were expected to squeeze into the 'popular' neighbourhoods of the eastern part of Paris – or, failing to find lodging there, to flee to the suburbs. They did so by the tens of thousands. Today Paris is a largely gentrified city surrounded by bleak suburbs to the north, east, and south that in time have become breeding-grounds of crime and social unrest.

To the public eye, Haussmann wrote large. Vast thoroughfares, monumental buildings, magnificent fountains – even his enormous network of sewage disposal and water supply – might come to mind at the mention of his name. What are often overlooked are his small contributions – the details – that together make for an agreeable life in a great city. From lighting fixtures to the little fences bordering the paths in his green spaces, Haussmann's hand is everywhere, largely unrecognised and strewn over the 20 *arrondissements* that compose Paris.

Is there no one place where the sheer variety of the prefect's works, great and small, can be grasped in a single visit? There is, and it happens to be a spot that also accurately reflects Haussmann's temperament. Within the confines of a few acres, he totally obliterated some of the most sinister pages of French history, creating in their place a source of pleasure and convenience for the living.

Let's go there.

Above: Baltard, the architect who designed the revolutionary central market of Paris, Les Halles, also created this church of Saint Augustin. The decorative stone exterior is only a 'skin' covering a skeleton of steel, the use of which material Baltard pioneered. Haussmann wanted a monument worthy of the entrance to his magnificent Boulevard Malesherbes, but the characteristics of the site forced Baltard to produce a rather deformed structure.

5
FROM HORROR TO HARMONY

PART 1

Below: On 12 March 1314, Jacques de Molay, commander of the Holy Order of the Knights Templar, was burned at the stake. So rich and powerful had the order become that King Philip the Fair ordered its destruction and shared its wealth with Pope Clement V.

Paris, 12 March 1314. From his palace facing the Place Dauphine, King Philippe IV, 'the Fair', looked down with satisfaction at the scene taking place below him. On the Ile des Juifs, a little island in the Seine, a man, Jacques de Molay, was about to be burned at the stake beside Guy, his brother. As the kindling flared, de Molay glared up at the King. The Grand Master of the suppressed order of the Knights Templars swore that they would soon meet again – in God's court of justice. Within months, Philippe, too, was dead.

Elsewhere, 54 Knights of the Temple were forced to confess to outrageous crimes, such as sacrilege, blasphemy and even, for good measure, sodomy. After hideous tortures, which included the pouring of molten lead into their ears, they, too, went to the stake. The burnings ended the power of a religious order so wealthy that it had virtually constituted a state within a state.

Ironically, Philippe's first glimpse of the wealth of the Templars came when he himself had sought protection in their fortress from the people of Paris who were rioting against a drastic currency devaluation. For the first time, the king grasped the extent of the treasury the Knights had accumulated. Not only had they been richly rewarded for their valour during the crusades in the Holy Land, but their holdings had swelled by inheritance and investment, particularly through the establishment of an international banking network. Their arrogance grew along with their power; the king found the combination unbearable.

Seeing such booty within his reach, Philippe had no difficulty winning the backing of Pope Clement V for a plan to destroy the order and to divide the proceeds. In fact, de Molay's invitation

to meet Philippe in the presence of the Supreme Judge in heaven had also been extended to Clement. Within the year, he, too, was liberated from his mortal coil, thus speeding his appearance before the celestial bar of justice.

The fortress of the Temple was de Molay's headquarters and a brooding incarnation of the medieval spirit, with its mysticism and its brutality. Covering acres of what was then the northern outskirts of Paris (today the 3rd *Arrondissement*), its massive walls were 24 feet high and pierced by only one entrance. Inside teemed a city capable of meeting all the needs, spiritual and temporal, of its inhabitants, and protected by a formidable military force. All told, 4,000

Right: The dungeon of the walled enclave of the Knights Templar. It was here that the royal family were held prisoners, until one by one, they climbed the steps to the guillotine. Only the boy Louis XVII escaped that fate. Instead, his care was entrusted to a cruel guard and he died, some say insane, of neglect and, perhaps, heartbreak. His end remains a mystery.

people lived within the compound – aristocrats, clerics and artisans, not to mention debtors who fled there to escape from their creditors. The entire population of the Temple, including the artisans and their production, was exempt from taxation – one of several reasons for Philippe's irritation. Another was the splendour of the Grand Master's palace which stood in the shadow of a dungeon, 90 feet high, that housed the rank-and-file of the Knights. The ensemble represented only a small part of the Templars' land holdings: they owned one-tenth of the city of Paris, including the entire Marais district, and property throughout Europe.

With the suppression of the Order of the Temple, the only important change was that a new order, the Knights of Malta, moved into the compound with the pope's blessing, while the wealth of the old order was divided between state (two-thirds) and church (one-third). Less important but more visibly hostile, the great outer walls of the fortress were eventually destroyed in 1667 and replaced by a more modest enclosure.

And so matters stood for the next 120 years, until the people of Paris caught the revolutionary fever of the late 18th century that already had inspired the Americans to rise up against their English king, George III. In France, Jacques de Molay's heavenly-directed curse against royalty and the pope had finally touched ground in the wrath that was unleashed on Louis XVI, his family and on the Church of Rome.

In 1792 the amiable but weak monarch was caught trying to flee from France with his retinue. Having brought the frustrated royals back to Paris under armed escort, the revolutionary Commune saw to it that there would be no further attempts at escape. The Temple, they reckoned, was ideally suited to thwart any conspiracy, outside or within its sinister walls. There the royal family was to be installed.

Nothing sinister, however, marked the reception of the Bourbons into the Temple. The magnificent palace of the Templars was still standing, though the reception committee no longer consisted of princes and bishops but rather of inhabitants of the *quartier* – workers, shopkeepers, artisans. A decent dinner was served and the guests were treated with courtesy. Louis XVI even discussed how he and his group would be lodged, assuming no doubt that this would also be in the palace.

Immediately after dinner, the atmosphere changed. Instead of being treated as 'guests', the visitors suddenly found that they had become prisoners. That same evening, 13 August 1792, they were led to the dungeon. All was ready. The vast bare floor spaces of the tower had been divided into four rooms at each level. In this rude accommodation, the family spent its last days together. The youngest, and most important member in terms of the future of France, was Louis, the son of Louis XVI and Marie-Antoinette. His schooling went on, conducted by his mother and her sister, Madame Elisabeth, as though he were being groomed to, one day, rule the nation as Louis XVII. For company, the prince, seven years old, had a sister, Madame Royale, who was fourteen.

On 21 January 1793, the revolutionary militia came to free the king from his captivity. Outside a tumbrel awaited while one of history's most pathetic partings took place between the doomed king and his loved ones. For two hours the open wagon bearing the king circulated the boulevards to give the mobs ample opportunity to jeer their monarch on his way to the scaffold at the north-east corner of the Place de la Révolution. He died bravely. The square later came to be named Place de la Concorde in an effort to scrub from memory the rivers of blood that had drenched its stones. However, on the façade of the Hôtel Crillon, passers-by can still find the old name, Place Louis XVI, preserved under glass.

Above: The arrival of the royal family at the palace of the Grand Prior of the Temple. They were well received, wined and dined, but then were shown to their 'guest suite' – in the dungeon tower.

On the morning after the king's execution, the three royal women kneeled and swore fealty to their new king, Louis XVII. Five months later the boy was taken away from his mother and removed to another floor where he was placed in the custody of a brutal caretaker named Simon. On 1 August the Commune removed the queen to the Conciergerie on the left bank of the Seine where she endured two-and-a half months of loneliness and humiliation at the hands of her guards before being decapitated on 16 October.

After 21 months of captivity in the Temple, Madame Elisabeth in her turn was led to the guillotine. The last of a tumbrel-load of 21 women to mount the scaffold, she pleaded with her executioner not to remove the scarf that covered her breasts: 'In the name of God, sir,' she cried, 'do not expose me.'

As for the dauphin, the child who was born to rule France, the last days of his short life must have been even more terrible than those of his parents and his aunt. The exact date of his death and the events leading to it remain mysteries for scholars to grapple with. It is clear, none the less, that his treatment at the hands of M. Simon and his wife was extremely cruel – combining neglect and punish-

ment – very likely at the urging of their revolutionary employers. One visitor reported seeing a boy of Louis's age – his tangled hair uncut, his skin covered with scabs and his eyes rolling in madness. To send a child to the scaffold might have offered a more horrifying spectacle than even the most hardened veterans of those bloody days could countenance. Yet for them it was equally unthinkable to allow the inheritor of the throne to come of age in captivity, providing a rallying point during decades to come for the surviving royalists in France as well as for those who had emigrated.

Accordingly, Louis XVII simply disappeared. After the restoration of the monarchy in 1814, Louis XVIII showed little interest, perhaps understandably, in discovering the whereabouts of the young prince with his prior claim to the throne. Eventually human remains supposed to be his were found in a nearby cemetery, but they turned out to those of a man more than 20 years old. And so the story trails off – of a little boy who was used to every comfort the society of his times could offer, who no doubt was the darling of the women of his family as well as his father, and who was forced to watch as they were, one by one, dragged away to die and who then lived on, alone, to endure an even worse fate than the adults – one of neglect, cruelty and, finally, emaciated and half mad, death.

In the years that followed, some 43 persons came forward to assert that they were indeed the vanished Louis XVII. None could prove it.

Above: The imprisoned royal family under guard at dinner in the dungeon of the city of the former Knights Templar. At the head of the table: Louis XVI; to his right, Marie Antoinette; to his left, the future Louis XVII who died in captivity.

Above: The imperial and republican governments of nineteenth-century France were in rare agreement; the Temple, prison of Louis XVI and Marie Antoinette before they were guillotined, must not become a rallying point for royalists seeking the return of the monarchy. Thus the only surviving evidence of the vast Temple compound is this painting in the church of St Elisabeth on the opposite side of the Rue de Temple.

Fearing that the infamous dungeon would become a point of pilgrimage for royalists, in 1808 Napoleon I ordered the tower to be razed, and the site became an open-air market-place.

Only the palace of the Grand Master remained standing when Napoleon's nephew came to power. Illustrating the political swings and roundabouts of the first half of the 19th century, the building had been used as an ammunition magazine under the Commune and later as a convent under the restoration of the monarchy. In 1857 Napoleon III ordered the levelling of the site to be completed, and the long tragic history of the Temple ended.

This was the kind of destruction of the dark side of medieval Paris that the prefect Haussmann relished.

But what to do with the vast unoccupied space that would result?

PART 2

Paris, 1857. Haussmann never did anything partially except for the projects that were interrupted by his departure from public office and the ensuing Franco–Prussian War. He erased every ugly memory of the fortress of the Temple with a thoroughness that left only a small chunk of the base of the dungeon buried today in a workshop in the obscure Rue de Picardie (No. 32) in the north-east corner of the Marais district. Elsewhere only a pair of wooden gates survive from the carriage-way of the palace, having been removed to No. 1 Rue St-Claude (at the corner of the Rue de Turenne) where they still can be seen.

Despite the thoroughness with which Napoleon III and Haussmann scrubbed from the square all evidence of the grim events that transpired there, the city of Paris is today lavish with historical markers. Two of them, handsome shields mounted on stanchions at eye-level, recount the events that unfolded in the days of the Templars and during the Revolution.

What the visitor does see is a refuge from the clatter of traffic and the bustle of the nearby public market. Inside the Square du Temple he comes across an inventory of Haussmann's treatment of public spaces. The square demonstrates the prefect's attention to every aspect of a project. He threw the stars of his team into the task of replacing ugliness with beauty: in this case, the architects Hittorff, designer of the Gare du Nord; Baltard, whose central food market represented a new epoch in architecture; and Alphand, the landscape designer of the Bois de Boulogne and the Bois de Vincennes.

To name such giants is a risk. It conjures up large edifices and grand projects and overlooks Haussmann's interest in every detail. If grand thoroughfares and vast railway stations excited him, so too did fluted lamp-posts and handsome steel discs to protect the roots of his beloved trees. He regarded the big projects as the

Below: The Square du Temple looking east where the town hall of the 3rd Arrondissement was soon to replace the power station and its chimney.

structure of the city, while such matters as the design of park benches he saw as the furniture within the structure. In design and colour the 'furniture' of the Square du Temple is precisely the same as in dozens of other parks of Paris, whether it be this snug patch of greenery in a corner of the Marais district, or such a vast swathe of trees, water and turf as the park of Montsouris.

To enter or leave one neighbourhood park is to enter or leave them all. For example, from the Rue du Temple, the visitor passes through swinging gates of iron mesh, waist high, that flank a centre panel of the same design and dimensions. The gates are dark green, as is the fence surrounding the park as well as all the fixtures inside: lamp-posts, drinking-fountains and the ankle-high interlocking croquet-like wickets that protect the grass and the flower beds. The harmony between all of these elements is striking. For example, the park benches with their rounded backs are made of horizontal wooden slats, while the nearby rubbish bins are made from green strips of the same diameter, but these are of metal and flared outward at the top, the better to receive carelessly thrown refuse.

A later age might see these identical items, found everywhere in Paris, foreshadowing the rise of manufacturing by the use of interchangeable parts. Aside from the harmony they impose, Haussmann no doubt was aware of the economies latent in the production of identical objects. Both considerations would appeal to his orderly mind.

Below: The Square du Temple as it appeared in 1865 after the walled city of the Knights Templar was destroyed, including the dungeon where the royal family were imprisoned, as well as the church, the palace of the commander and all other buildings. Napoleon III sought to erase any reminder of the events that took place there lest it became a focal point for resurgent royalists.

A small green cabin inside and to the right of the entrance from the Avenue du Temple is the guardian's refuge where he can change into his uniform. His job consists largely of chasing evil-doers from setting foot on the grass and making clear to dog-owners that their pets are unwelcome in his domain. To the left of the gate is a businesslike tap which provides '*eau potable*' – drinking-water for visitors and residents – a reminder of the prefect's fresh-water fetish. Penetrating the park by a typical sand and gravel path, one comes quickly to the sand-pit, where small children play happily on slides and climb about wooden structures resembling the framework of houses.

At intervals bordering the circular path today are electric-arc street lights. Because Paris still awaited a city-wide network of lines to carry electricity, Haussmann's lighting was by gas, a vast improvement over the smoky oil lamps they replaced. Shelter, water ... food ... and lighting – all these basic necessities captured Haussmann's full attention. He had in his armoury 21 different shapes of street lamp, all crowning stanchions of uniform design. Here, atop the fluted bronze lamp-posts, Alphand chose globes of frosted glass – perhaps to carry on the circular pattern of the pathway through the park.

The prefect was by no means opposed to electrical lighting; his progressive nature would embrace it. As proof, he made full use of electric-arc flood-lighting to enable the work on his construction sites to continue by night. For the time being lamp-lighters with their long poles were needed at sunset and again at dawn.

Above: The eastern side of the Square du Temple as it appears today, with the borough hall of the 3rd Arrondissement dominating the scene.

Moving along, the visitor to the Square du Temple comes upon a peaceful little lake fed by a miniature waterfall emerging from a rocky dell. The work of Alphand, of course – except for the ducks whose quacking adds a bucolic note. Strangely, here, directly opposite the site of the destroyed palace, is a tortured tree overhanging the little lake, not very high but twisted and gnarled with age. It is called a weeping beech. Like a touch on the shoulder, its drooping branches are the only remaining hint of the tragedies that once cast their shadow over this corner of Paris.

Exiting on the side of the park opposite the entrance. the stroller confronts the work of the second star to whom Haussmann confided the transformation of this unhappily historic site. Hittorff's Hôtel de Ville of the 3rd *Arrondissement* may not be awe-inspiring or an architectural gem, but it is a solid and pleasing neo-classical building. And, once again, it embodies Haussmannian consistency in its kinship with the other five *mairies* constructed during his time in office.

To the left of the Hôtel de Ville stands the work that reflects a third genius – the architect Baltard. The large covered market of the Temple is one of only two remaining examples of his pioneering fusion of glass with ironwork. (See below for a discussion of the other one – the great hall of La Villette.) For a local market, that of the Temple is huge. Curiously, it shelters not only food stands, but also a large area devoted to the sale of clothing of good quality at reasonable prices. Two great halls at right angles to the Rue Eugène-Spillier are linked by a smaller third hall, each of them lighted by a peaked glass roof. The structure is supported by great iron stanchions, and the walls and ceilings are also of glass. In summer the great doors can be rolled open. All these features, particularly the bonding of iron to glass, are reminders of the lamented Marché des Halles, now replaced by the claustrophobic Forum des Halles, an underground shopping mall only a stone's throw from the Pompidou Museum, said to be the most visited attraction in Paris. The 'Centre Beaubourg', as the Pompidou is called by Parisians, is as structurally honest as the former Baltard market-place. Far from concealing its skeletal structure and life-support systems such as ventilators and elevators, it flaunts them in brilliant colours.

The Marché du Temple is not only a reminder of Baltard's originality but also of Haussmann's determination to render more efficient the distribution of fresh food throughout the capital. Baltard's gigantic wholesale market was designed to be the central point of the system – a function it fulfilled until 1969 when the growth of the city spawned such congestion around what Zola called the 'belly of Paris' that the central market was transferred to Rungis, eight miles south of the metropolis. (An important consideration in the decision to move the operation out of Paris was health and sanitation, jeopardised by the attraction left-over food particles held for rats, cockroaches and less visible creatures.)

Similar concerns prompted Haussmann to relegate to the northern edge of the city the route travelled by animals on their way to the slaughter-houses of Paris. Beasts too large to be transported by wagon – such as cows and horses – were driven to their doom through the narrow medieval streets, adding to the odorif-

Left: Not wishing to revive royalist sentiments, the Second Empire under Napoleon III wanted to efface the memory of the events that unfolded in the Temple. This modest plaque on the façade of the borough hall of the 3rd Arrondissement is situated well above the gaze of passers-by. It reads simply: 'Here stood the dungeon of the Temple where Louis XVI and the royal family were imprisoned beginning 13 August 1792.' What happened afterwards is left unmentioned.

erous compost already rotting on the pavement. Given Haussmann's horror of filth, getting rid of the animals was high on his list. As always, he tolerated no half-measures. Once again, he called on Baltard's technique of marrying glass and iron to produce the ventilation and light required in a slaughter-house. The building, in what is now the 19th *Arrondissement* boasts the largest roof surface in Paris, making it ideal, today, for simultaneous entertainment and musical events.

Aside from being a reminder of Baltard's work, the Marché du Temple also happens to serve as a reminder of Haussmann's essential role as an intermediary between the Emperor, with his highly generalised ideas, and the creative people whose job it was to turn them into reality. The story of Les Halles goes back more than a decade before Haussmann's arrival as prefect in 1853. Already an important outdoor market, it was not easily reached by the well-heeled residents of the Marais district to the east. Always attentive to the needs of the moneyed class, King Louis-Philippe, Louis Napoleon's predecessor, ordered his prefect to crash through the tangle of crooked streets separating the Marais from the market. The result was the historically important Rue Rambuteau, named for the prefect of that time. It has the distinction of being the first great Paris street created through the expropriation of private property. Unaware, King Louis-Philippe had within his grasp the key to the modernisation of Paris. What he lacked was the inner fire which drove two Napoleons to get on with the renovation of the city. The new prefect, Haussmann, picked up the key and turned it with the concept of value-added as a basis for financing the reconstruction. After that, all became possible.

Berger, Rambuteau's successor and the predecessor of Haussmann, was close-fisted when it came to public spending. But he realised that, with the opening of the Rue Rambuteau, Les Halles had become a vital centre that required a proper shelter. He engaged as architect none other than Baltard – and with disastrous results. Baltard's building, looking like a stone fortress, was already well started when Louis Napoleon became Emperor. He, quite simply, ordered the destruction of the building, leaving the newly appointed Haussmann to deal with a predictably furious Baltard. It's hard to imagine a more explosive mixture of power and creativity than that which existed between the Emperor and the architect. Happily Haussmann and Baltard had been childhood friends. Earlier, when the new prefect had overturned the eminent Hittorff's plans for what today is the Avenue Foch, Haussmann had wielded blatant authority. But there was an important difference between the two situations; Hittorff had not already *built* something, only to see it destroyed. This time the prefect sought a way to persuade the talented Baltard to start again. Remembering Napoleon III's attempts to sketch a structure to make clear his objections to Baltard's first attempt, Haussmann hit on the word 'parasols' – perhaps picked up from conversation with the Emperor. Umbrellas, not masonry, were what were needed. Light, ventilation, freedom of movement. In short, structures that would capture the ambience of an open-air market and at the same time avoid clashing with the buildings surrounding the area.

Happily, Baltard sparked to the idea, and went on to design six structures eminently suited to their purpose that would become legendary as engineering feats. When the plan for their destruction in 1961 came to light, it created a brouhaha in creative and intellectual circles in Paris and elsewhere. To no avail. Today only wispy lattice-like ghosts of Baltard's work decorate the gardens of the Halles. One of the original 'halls' was, however, re-assembled in nearby Nogent-sur-Marne where it can be seen today.

Later Baltard renewed his devotion to structural ironwork, but overlaid it with a pastiche of rococo stonework that emerged as the Church of St-Augustin at the threshold of the Boulevard Malesherbes in the 8th *Arrondissement*.

Circling back along the northern side of the Square du Temple, one arrives at the junction of the Rue de Perrée and the Rue du Temple. Here the stroller can see yet another example of Haussmannian innovation. All over Paris today one finds what are called (after their inventor) Morris columns. The cylindrical surface of these columns are perfect for displaying colourful theatre advertisements. Today they continue to do the job; some even rotating to help the weary passer-by catch up with the latest spectacles without budging.

On the opposite side of the Rue du Temple from the park, at No. 195, stands the church of Ste-Elisabeth, built by Catherine de Médicis. Inside is a plaque which proclaims: 'This church is the centre of religious services for the Society of the Order of Knights of Malta.' And so the occupants of the Temple who

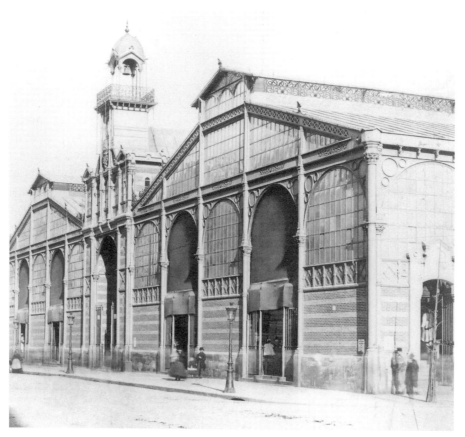

Left and right: The iron-and-glass innovations of Baltard, the pioneering architect of the lamented central market of Paris ('Les Halles'), are preserved today in the Marché du Temple. Built also under Haussmann, it was two-thirds destroyed, in 1903. In the existing part, fashionable, high-quality leather garments are on sale among other items, at bargain prices.

succeeded the Templars live on in the *quartier*, though far less ostentatiously than they did from the 13th to the 18th centuries.

It is only a five-minute stroll from the Church of Ste-Elisabeth to the gigantic hub that is the Place de la République with its twelve intersecting streets, avenues and boulevards (as well as, today, its six Métro stations). The modest dwellings that surround the République proclaim that this is an unpretentious neighbourhood, far removed from the elegance of those adjacent to the Etoile. But when it comes to the public spaces in all parts of the city, equality triumphs; Parisians living in the eastern *arrondissements* have just as easy access to the Bois de Vincennes as have the bourgeoisie to the west to their nearby Bois de Boulogne.

In terms of spaciousness, the Place de la Nation, only 500 yards from the Bois de Vincennes, rivals the more frequently visited Etoile with its incomparable Arc de Triomphe. Both parks became playgrounds for all Paris after being linked by the opening of the first Métro line (Line No. 1 – holed through in 1886). Even more effectively than Haussmann's broad Rue St-Antoine and the Rue de Rivoli, the inauguration of Line 1 linked east and west – just as later lines would tie all *arrondissements* into what is arguably the world's most efficient urban transport system.

The opening in 1990 of the gigantesque Opéra de la Bastille spurred the intermingling of east and west in the Place de la Bastille, midway between La République and La Nation. Planned as the 'poor man's Opéra', the Bastille today is just as pricey as the superb 'Palais Garnier' situated in the very centre of Paris. However, the visitor to the Place can enjoy without charge the site of the birthplace of the Revolution as well as the pre-Haussmann intimacy of the neighbourhood's winding streets. But be warned: their days are likely to be limited; signs, 'permission to demolish' and 'permission to construct', are festooning many peeling walls, heralding the arrival of gentrification.

If there is one area of Paris that seems somewhat cheated in the bestowal of green spaces, it is it is the opposite side of the Seine. As a student on the Left Bank, Haussmann grumbled about the dilapidation of the university area. Later he took his revenge by slicing through the tangle of alleys and one-way streets with two great north-south thoroughfares to supplement the existing, but narrow, Rue du Faubourg St-Jacques – the Boulevard St-Michel and the Avenue du Maine. Essential, too, was the creation of an east-west link, the Rue des Ecoles. To make up for the shortage of snug parks, he more than compensated by creating, with his friend Alphand, the lovely Parc de Montsouris (See chapter 3) in the 14th *Arrondissement*.

The nearby Rue Monge in the 5th *Arrondissement* is also a result of the prefect's transformations on the Left Bank. A few steps to the east is a hidden refuge, a swatch of greenery that surrounds some remarkable vestiges of the Roman city of Lutetia (Lutce). Here at least Haussmann resurrected, rather than erased, antiquity. It was the construction of the Rue Monge that brought to light the Roman arena where 2,000 years ago, gladiators fought and theatrical performances were mounted for the diversion of the settlers of Paris. It is a fair guess that Haussmann was thrilled with his discovery. His speeches were peppered with allusions to the Roman Empire and its glories. The link between the two civilisations – Caesar's and Louis Napoleon's – was a constant theme in his devotion to broad thoroughfares, elegant perspectives and grand monuments. Hadn't he made his point clearly, at the opening of the Avenue Malesherbes when he said: 'Here in Paris, the nephew of Caesar has revived the imperial city, above all, to further the well-being of his subjects.' How more 'imperial' can one get?"

Here, as in every park, the elegant gas lamps (now, of course, electrified), the park benches, the fences, all bear the stamp of Haussmann with his insistence on weaving the Paris 'furniture' as well as its monuments, into the cohesive urban tapestry that is uniquely Paris. Perhaps he had in mind a more pragmatic goal than harmony alone. In 1860, seven years after Haussmann moved into the Hôtel de Ville, the Emperor signed a decree that doubled the land area of the city.

His stroke of the pen confronted his more than willing prefect with all the problems of integrating into Paris eight disparate suburbs with different modes of living and differing levels of economic welfare. The spiritual distance between white-collar Passy and blue-collar Belleville was infinitely greater than the breadth of Paris that separated them. The articles of urban furniture that Haussmann and his team introduced soon became trademarks of the renewed city. As such, they played an important role of unification. Whether one seeks refuge in the calm of the gardens of the Ranelagh or is strolling along the Rue Ménilmontant, one finds oneself not just in Passy or Belleville, but, unmistakably, in Paris. The outdoor structures knit together a city where people tend to identify first with their *quartier*, secondly with their *arrondissement*, and then as residents of the Left or Right Bank. The trademarks Haussmann developed for Paris are useful reminders that, whatever their address, they are, after all, Parisians.

By what magic did Haussmann in a mere seventeen years achieve the visual harmony so evident throughout the length and breadth of the city? One must keep in mind that, while his talents as an administrator bloomed in Paris, they were nurtured through twenty years of exposure to an astonishing variety of challenges and opportunities. First as the humble general secretary of the prefecture of Poitiers, he mastered the routine business of speeding paperwork and arriving at decisions – among the dullest, but at the same time one of the essential activities of a bureaucratic administrator. Yet, in mountainous Yssingeaux the young sub-prefect showed a surprising flare for bringing together fiercely opposed factions for the common good. His eight years in Nérac stirred his passion for liberating transport by building roads and bridges, even while he vastly increased literacy by establishing schools. Even his 'exile' to St-Girons in the Pyrenees would later prove profitable; it renewed his interest in hydrology and provided final proof of his stamina and courage. Later, in Blaye and Bordeaux, he honed his political talents by successfully negotiating with honour two critical turning points in French history. It was also in Bordeaux that he was seduced by a city that became for him a model of urban beauty. All this was reinforced later by two impressive exercises in achieving civic order – once in the Var and again in Auxerre.

It adds up to an impressive résumé, but a good career history fails to explain the feats Haussmann was able to perform. To be sure, the mastery of so many different kinds of challenges refined him into a highly skilled administrator. Such figures have long been a key to the continuing progress of a France prone to political upheavals. They are expert in deciphering the maze of laws and regulations that encrust any bureaucracy but are equally adroit in the uses of power. Charles de Gaulle was merely underlining their importance when, immediately after the Second World War, he established the National School of Administration as the highest standard of education for public service – a graduate school accessible only to the brightest students after rigorous preparation. Haussmann's school was the prefectorial network that in France permitted (as to a lesser degree it still does) the state to participate directly in the affairs of every *département* and county of France. Under an Emperor this meant that a prefect wielded immense power. The direct line of absolute authority from Napoleon III to his prefect made possible the rebuilding of Paris. With it, Haussmann was able to delegate to his chosen lieutenants the authority that they needed in order to swing swiftly into action.

And – a vital part of his success – he chose his aides well. In the matter of implanting the outdoor furniture of Paris, his squad was headed by Davioud. In terms of architecture, it was Baltard; landscaping, Alphand; engineering, Belfond. Except for Davioud, each man was well known to Haussmann before he became prefect – Baltard, a former schoolmate; Alphand from the Bordeaux days; Belfond from Auxerre. Today, all have their monuments – or streets bearing their names.

In brief, Haussmann was a superb judge of men.

Yet his qualifications alone cannot explain his prodigious capacity for work and his drive to push through to concrete results. The missing element can be found in his almost fanatical likes and dislikes – call them his loves and hatreds. He loved pure air and hated the poisonous atmosphere of a medieval Paris that, it was said, almost destroyed his lungs. He loved cleanliness and hygiene with a passion intriguing to a psychologist – and he hated dirt of any kind, whether in the environment or in a person. Above all, he loved order – in administration as well as in architecture and the planning of streets. In fact, his hatred of the clutter of old Paris was so visceral that he frequently had to be restrained when he tried to demolish buildings of a certain merit. Nobody, however, tried to stop his destruction of his childhood home in the 8th *Arrondissement* at the corner of the Faubourg St-Honoré and today's Boulevard Haussmann. (This act triggered the usual volley of invective. 'How soulless', was the cry. Very likely the shrillness would have been ear-splitting if he had saved his parental homestead while the houses of others were crashing down on all sides.)

Clearly, it's impossible to portray the personality and character of the baron in pastels. This impossibility tells us much. It implies the existence of an immense ego – one that can literally move mountains when abetted by direct access to imperial power. However, it also implies a supreme confidence in the rightness of his decisions. But he was not always right. Suppose, for example, that Napoleon III was finding it necessary to modify his dictatorial style in favour of more give-and-take with his senators and deputies. In that case, what happens if his No. 1 lieutenant persists in the use of strong-arm methods? Exactly that was fast becoming a reality. Yet the baron – his head full of projects as yet unrealised – appears to have missed the signals – or simply chose to ignore them.

The sound of the verbal artillery Haussmann's enemies had never before dared to use began to resound in the halls of the *parlement*, the time for settling old scores was at hand and the prefect was directly in the line of fire.

6
THE PRICE
OF GLORY

PART 1

'Within Haussmann there were two men (or, better, two aspects of the same man). There was the dedicated man, hard-working and self-sacrificing, alongside the man self-satisfied and boastful, attracted to the pomp of Catholicism with its colour and audacious authority, yet steeped in the austere Protestantism to which he was profoundly committed. He was the Puritan, deeply attached to the loyal and devoted Madame Haussmann who often found herself eclipsed by the pretty faces of the time, so alluring to an ageing man. And then there was the private man, content with his intimate circle of friends yet yoked to the showman fond of conducting the most glorious public festivities of the Empire.

'From one to the other of these two men it was only a step.'*

Paris 1869. The prefect who had moved mountains of earth and slain the dragon of cholera had long resolved also to change the magnetic pole of Paris. His proposed location of the new opera house made Haussmann's intention clear. In planning the three successive stages of the reconstruction of Paris, the baron's admiration for Bordeaux was never far from his mind. Especially present was the image of Bordeaux's Grand Théâtre. In terms of city planning, the auditorium of Victor Louis was, for all its magnificence, more than just a sumptuous place of entertainment; it stood as the focal point of the city's network of handsome boulevards – and therefore of the city itself.

So it would be in Paris.

For more than 1,000 years the city's heart had been in the Ile de la Cité. To the dismay of many, Haussmann ruthlessly levelled most of the dwellings on that cramped island, disengaging Notre-Dame Cathedral (at the time being restored by the controversial architect, Viollet-le-Duc) from a clutter of dilapidated buildings. Other great structures remained, all redolent of French history. They included the Palais de Justice, the Ste-Chapelle of King Saint Louis, and the Conciergerie (remembered by most people as the notorious prison where Marie-Antoinette and other aristocrats awaited their turn to die under the knife of the guillotine.) At the same time, the Cité became the site of the new Tribunal de Commerce, the rebuilt

---

* G.-N. Lameyre. *Haussmann, Préfet de Paris*. Flammarion, Paris, 1958.

Hôtel Dieu hospital and all the buildings that remained on the island owed their presence to tradition. (As an institution, even the Tribunal de Commerce pre-dated Napoleon I and is, in fact, the oldest continuing court of justice in France.)

Yet Haussmann, as always, was looking more to the future than to the past. The railway, department stores, cafés and entertainment – all represented the new Paris and all were flourishing to the north and the west of Notre-Dame. At the same time, the destruction of hundreds of unstable dwellings reduced the population of the Ile by an estimated 70 per cent. Although the roots of the Cité remained alive, they were no longer capable of sustaining a flourishing community life.

Haussmann had proposed the site of the new Opéra at the height of his powers in 1860. He encountered no opposition from a review board which he himself had appointed. In any case, the people 'who counted' – meaning the rich and the aristocratic – were hardly likely to object, since the proposed building fronted on the Boulevard des Capucines – one of the three 'Grands Boulevards' that they viewed as their special heritage. Created under Louis X1V, these linked, tree-lined boulevards probably won the appellation 'Grand' because, before Haussmann's arrival, they formed the only pleasant promenades in the city. Stretching from either end of the Boulevard des Capucines are the Boulevard de la Madeleine to the west and the Boulevard des Italiens to the east. An invisible sign saying 'no overalls allowed' on the three boulevards shielded the rich, during their Sunday stroll, from the poor, who in any case lived a safe distance away – well to the east.

If the sedate Boulevard des Capucines formed the front yard of the projected Opera House, the area behind the building was anything but snobbish. The streets around the Chaussée d'Antin were alive with traffic, on foot and horse-drawn. People thronged the dazzling new department stores – Les Galeries Lafayette and Le Printemps. Well-heeled visitors to Paris gravitated to the luxurious hotels – notably the Grand and the Scribe – that were springing up nearby. By 1869, the last year that Haussmann was in office, 1,300,000 passengers a day passed through the handsome Gare St-Lazare. Since its trains served the western part of the city and the suburbs beyond, the great station testified to the westward shift of the inhabitants. (To appreciate today the elegance of the main hall of the terminal, the visitor must imagine its walls stripped of the billboards and ticket-vending machines that radically alter its countenance.)

The Main Street of all this bustle? The Boulevard Haussmann which remained uncompleted in 1868 even though construction of the Opéra had begun six years earlier (and would continue for another seven years.) The boulevard ended at the Chaussée d'Antin and then resumed a few yards to the west, at the junction of the Rue Taitbout. Sensing perhaps that his star was waning, Haussmann moved to close the gap. As a result, opera-goers – and Haussmann himself was among the most enthusiastic of them - would be able to approach the new opera house from either end of 'his' boulevard. As we have seen, work at the same time was nearing its climax in the creation of the vast water-supply system – perhaps Haussmann's greatest contribution to the well-being of the city. Nevertheless, this little scrap of

125

paving, only 200 metres long, had an importance of its own; it was the last street to be completed under Haussmann's direction.

For 21 years after his enemies pried him out of office, Haussmann lived an active life, the latter part of it in a modest apartment at No. 12 Rue Boissy d'Anglas where he worked on his mammoth three-volume memoirs. Perhaps towards the end he even savoured a special kind of recognition that neither he nor anyone else could have foreseen. Despite the visibility of writers who vied with Victor Hugo in attacking Haussmann's work, exercising their craft to express their distaste for the baron's work – branding him, in effect, a Philistine – another group of creative people were gravitating to the area just north of the Gare St-Lazare, only a brief walk from his apartment. Perhaps because they were painters, they were able to look at Paris with a fresh eye – the gaze of Impressionism. The first artist of note to settle in the area near the Place de l'Europe was Gustave Caillebotte who lived there with his parents. He came to appreciate the special light and especially his large Hauss-mannian room which gave him the working space he needed.

Caillebotte, a naval architect by profession, praised the area to his artist friends. He himself found much to paint there – the Place de l'Europe itself as well as the iron bridge over the railway lines. Claude Monet, living in Argenteuil, came often to Paris, arriving at the Gare St-Lazare. He, too found himself attracted by the new cityscape – so much so that Caillebotte, whose family was well-off, rented a studio for him at 17 Rue de Moncey (now the Rue de Berne). Nearby, in a modest studio overlooking the railway lines, Edouard Manet painted eleven canvases, among them his famous views of a train arriving at the station. At least ten other painters, including Berthe Morisot, set up their easels in the neighbour-hood. Emile Zola understood: 'Our painters today must find poetry in railway stations just as their fathers found it in forests and rivers.'

As for Haussmann, music was the art he understood, and cherished all of his life. Aside from that, he poured his special creativity into the creation of the new city of Paris – and into the spectacular public festivities and galas which he staged with the sure hand of a born showman.

Based on the evidence, it is clear that the painters of the day appreciated the significance of Haussmann's transformations far more readily than he was equipped to see what they were reaching for. To his way of thinking, Impres-sionism must have represented a lamentable lack of precision.

Even a prefect fully backed by the power of an Emperor can find himself checkmated. The baron left office with one major problem unsolved. It was quite literally a grave problem: the lack of space for burying the dead. The cemeteries of Montmartre and Montparnasse were filled. Père Lachaise contained 74,000 sepulchres. Yet the population of Paris continued to swell, and the crowding of the burial grounds was posing severe problems of contamination of the underground water sources. Certainly, without the new sources of drinking-water created by Haussmann and his engineer Belgrand, a sinister problem would have become an intolerable situation. Now one conclusion became inescapable: new lodgings for the dead, as well as for the living, had to be created.

Right: Haussmann at the time of his disgrace. To the city of Paris, he says: 'Is it possible, after I have loved you so, covered you with pearls and diamonds, and made you, so ugly before, the most beautiful woman in the world, that you should spurn me? Ungrateful woman!' He is shown pocketing an engagement ring.

PRIX DU NUMÉRO POUR PARIS ET LES DÉPARTEMENTS

Quatrième année. — N° 3

Samedi 15 Janvier 1870

25 centimes

PARIS-COMIQUE

JOURNAL ILLUSTRÉ

DIRECTEUR
CARLO GRIPP

ADMINISTRATION
6, Cité Trévise.

ABONNEMENTS: Paris, Six mois, 6 fr. Un an, 10 fr. Départements, Six mois, 7 fr. Un an, 12 fr. Les abonnements partent des 1er et 15 de chaque mois.

M. HAUSSMANN ET Mlle LUTÉCE

Est-il possible qu'après vous avoir tant aimée, qu'après vous avoir couverte de perles et de diamants, et fait
de vous, jadis si laide, la plus belle... fille de la terre, vous me disiez... zut! Ingrate!!!

Haussmann argued long and lucidly that the time of action had come. He appointed a commission, headed by Belgrand, to make recommendations. The group's report called for the creation of a large new burial ground near Pontoise, north of the city, to which the contents of the existing graves would be transferred.

A similar transfer had been made in 1785 under Louis XVI when thousands of remains were removed from the Cemetery of the Innocents near Les Halles to a labyrinth of abandoned quarries, 'the Catacombs'. This vast underground tomb is near the Place Denfert-Rochereau in today's 14th *Arrondissement*. There the bones of tens of thousands of the dispossessed are artistically arranged in geometric patterns. Should the visitor somehow escape the message communicated by so many grinning skulls, a sign every few yards is there to remind him of the fleeting nature of mortal existence. 'Look upon these bones and know that they once wore flesh and blood like you, just as you will soon become as one of them.' Climbing the stairs to the fresh air of the Avenue René Coty is a welcome exercise.

Because the earlier grisly removal had gone smoothly, Haussmann and Belgrand may have been lulled into thinking that their new plan would be accepted without important opposition. They were wrong. Suddenly everyone, it seemed, rallied round the dead. Ordinary citizens led the charge: 'Isn't it enough for M. Haussmann to dispossess the living? Now he wants to evict the dead.' Or, 'Monsieur le préfet: All the nations of the world respect their dead, even those we call uncivilised.' Writers sharpened their pens. Tracts with such titles as 'The Exile of the Dead; Paris without Cemeteries' appeared.

Above: The caption reads: 'The Winds of March (regarding rumours of the disgrace of Monsieur Haussmann)'. Nine months later, 2 January 1870, he was fired.

This uprising was unlike the fuss that greeted Haussmann's plan to snip off a corner of the Luxembourg Gardens. That was, basically, a squabble over aesthetics. This proposal struck a deep vein of love and grief. Furthermore, Napoleon III finally was beginning to reach out for the support of the people, permitting more expression, through their representatives, of their wishes. This time the Emperor failed to back his prefect, who may himself have lacked enthusiasm for this particular battle. After all, he also respected the dead.

The matter was dropped, only to be resurrected 60 years later when a new Parisian cemetery was dedicated just north of the city near the suburb of St-Ouen. During those six decades, piecemeal solutions – mostly in the form of modest additions to existing burial grounds – were improvised until the basic problem finally had to be dealt with. One thing is clear: without Haussmann's aqueducts which brought uncontaminated water into the city, the number of dead from cholera would have forced an earlier solution to the problem.

Despite the stalemate and despite the increased carping of his critics, Haussmann's special relation with Napoleon III continued. The baron stuck a deep chord within the Emperor through an initiative that regarded the past rather than the future. He appointed a commission to gather together every available document, text and historical record bearing on the history of the city of Paris. This work took five years to complete. Napoleon was thrilled with the results. 'Thanks to your efforts', he wrote Haussmann, 'the Paris of today is the most splendid and the most sanitary of all of the European capitals.' He closed with his personal regards.

The collection formed the basis of the Musée Historique de la ville de Paris in the Hôtel Carnavalet, the magnificent former residence of Madame de Sévigné. (Today a vastly expanded collection is housed in an annexe to the 16th-century Hôtel Lamoignon, 24 Rue Pavée, close to the Carnavalet.)

For the moment, at least, Haussmann had reason to feel that his situation was solidly anchored. He was, as a result, able to harness his considerable energy and enthusiasm to organising one of the great affairs of the time – the Universal Exhibition of 1867. The world was talking of the transformation of Paris, and the Who's Who of the world came to see for themselves. It would probably be easier to list the European royalty who were absent than those who flocked to the resplendent new capital. The Sultan of Constantinople, the Queen of Holland, the Archduke of Austria, the King and Queen of Portugal, Bismarck of Prussia – all were received at the Hôtel de Ville.

Among all the festivities, the banquet attended by the two Emperors, Napoleon III and Franz-Joseph, was certainly the most splendid. As usual on great occasions, the guests of honour were received by Haussmann at the foot of the grand staircase of the Hôtel de Ville while Octavie waited to greet them at the top. Reading the menu of the seven-course banquet which followed – beginning with soup and hot hors-d'oeuvres, proceeding through fish, meat and fowl, to end finally with pineapple in an oriental sauce – is bound to leave the modern diet-conscious diner with mental indigestion.

Afterwards, it was Haussmann of course who led the honoured guests to the dance floor, forcing a broad swathe through the packed assembly. 'Forgive me, ladies,' he announced, 'but you understand that in Paris we like our thoroughfares to be wide. Let the polka begin.'

The prefect was tireless. No wonder the British Press dubbed him 'Haussmann, the Magnificent.' He himself liked to say: 'It's astonishing how much can be accomplished if your workday begins at 6 a.m. and ends after midnight.'

Was there any honour that eluded him? There was one, but the void would soon be filled. Seven days after the closing of the exhibition, he was elected a Member of the Académie des Beaux-Arts.

If Haussmann's biography had been in the hands of a Hollywood director, no doubt the film would have ended on this note. He had all the titles and decorations

HAUSSMANN
Recéleur de PARIS vendu
a la Destruction.

Left: One example of the bitter political attacks against Haussmann. The text reads: "HAUSSMANN 'Profiteer from his destruction of Paris' 'THE PILLORY' 'Thief' (on Haussmann's forehead) The attempt to make the Protestant Haussmann appear to be Jewish adds one more unsavoury touch.

that even his hungry ego could ask for. More substantially, his projects were either firmly established or well on the way to fruition. Triumphant, he could simply have walked off the stage to applause – partly from those who recognised and appreciated his prodigious work and also from those who were glad to see him go. Unfortunately such a scenario would have run counter to Haussmann's character. The baron was a man with a mission. Such people never quit – until left with no choice.

PART 2

Paris 1870. The new Opera House was unfinished, as was the broad boulevard, the Avenue de l'Opéra, that was to lead to it. Among other projects still under way was the Boulevard Arago – an important link on the left bank between Denfert-Rochereau and the Boulevard de Port-Royal. Furthermore, only one of his two great reservoirs was in operation, though the second, Montsouris, was nearing completion. So many other projects were either in the early stages of construction or simply on paper that a contemporary actuarial table (if such existed) would have guided him; he could never hope to see 'his' Paris completed – except in his imagination.

What is bewildering about his stubbornness is Haussmann's failure to read the signs of the times. The skilled politician, who rode successive waves of social upheaval in France to arrive at the heights of power, seems to have been unaware of the mighty cross-currents which were now threatening to drag him down. After tolerating sixteen years of noise, dirt and disruption, the people of Paris were ready to enjoy the fruits of their patience without being asked to endure more of the same. For many, the fruits simply did not exist. Paris was jammed with itinerant construction workers attracted from all over France by the prospect of employment. To this floating work force was added that part of the population dispossessed by the demolitions. Many of the homeless found lodgings, not in the handsome buildings lining the boulevards, but behind them in courtyards where tawdry blocks of tenement housing were erected by the promoters to squeeze an extra profit from their expropriated land. But even these sombre flats could not meet the demand. Eventually, of course, most of the labourers from the provinces returned home while masses of Parisians were shoved into the peripheral suburbs. Inner-city decay was avoided but at a high cost – that of 'outer-city' desolation, still so evident today.

Another cross-current – and the most dangerous of all – was a growing suspicion of Haussmann's financial wizardry. With the Emperor's assent, he had set up an intricate system of banking operations whereby construction projects could be immediately financed and set in motion. A miracle! The new magnificence of Paris apparently would cost the Parisian tax-payers nothing. They were usually ignorant of the soaring indebtedness of such institutions as the so-called 'Crédit Foncier' and the 'Bank of Public Works'. Only an absolute faith that the loans to entrepreneurs could be repaid through an ever-increasing added-value of improved properties could justify the risks Haussmann had taken on behalf of the public.

Haussmann's authoritative, some said overbearing, manner didn't help. Napoleon III read the will of the public far better than did his lieutenant. He was continuing to soften the edges of his own imperial manner. As early as 1860, he gave his government a clear signal to this effect – one that impacted Haussmann directly. The prefect of the Seine had pushed the Emperor to name him 'Minister of Paris', thus gathering all functions of the city under his authority. His proposal wasn't simply a scheme for self-aggrandisement; it was a logical move to reflect the reality of Haussmann's influence. Eliminating his repeated skirmishes with the prefect of police and certain obstructionist ministers, the new title would have helped him get on with his job. Haussmann was not entirely on an ego trip; efficiency was his god.

Still co-operative, Napoleon III put the proposition before his ministers. In a clear warning of more opposition to come, they voted down the change. For once, the Emperor accepted their veto. He substituted a compromise measure which increased Haussmann's authority in scattered functions of city management but failed to change his title.

Five years later, the prefect demonstrated that he had not received the message that flexibility was in, strong-arm tactics out; to increase the voice of Parisians in the management of their city, Napoleon III named a new municipal council. Haussmann confronted it aggressively, hectoring the group in his best schoolmaster form. 'You cannot', he declared, 'regard Paris as some ordinary community. It is something entirely apart; it is a great capital. Paris belongs to the whole of France.' With these words, he downgraded the role of the city council, while inflating that of the national government. Clearly at odds with the Emperor's effort to democratise the decision-making process, he was making it easier for the opposition to single him out as their target. They could then go after their real quarry, a weakened Napoleon III.

The third current was scandal. Haussmann liked pretty women, especially those who danced or sang at the Opéra. Attacks on his personal life formed a juicy counterpoint to innuendoes about his honesty.

All three of these currents – his financial manipulations, his uncontrolled use of power, and his highly publicised infidelity to the much-loved Octavie – churned up a rising tide of criticism that threatened to engulf him. Few people could have breasted the tide with more intelligence – and dignity – than he.

His way of raising funds was at once a dazzling display of financial sophistication and at the same time his most vulnerable point. All the opposition lacked in 1869 was a charismatic spokesman to set alight the powder chain. They found one in the person of Jules Ferry, a brilliant young lawyer and sworn enemy of the Second Empire from the start. He not only had the words but enough ability with figures to permit him to thread his way through the intricacies of Haussmannian finance. In sounding the alarm, Ferry was helped enormously by the witty title of his treatise. At this time the play 'The Tales of Hoffmann', was at the peak of its success in Paris. In French, the title was 'Les Comptes Fantastiques d'Hoffmann'. Conveniently, the word *comptes* can mean both 'tales' and 'accounts'. So Ferry came up with his title, *'Les comptes fantastiques d'Haussmann'*. Few people found their way through Ferry's thicket of figures, but Paris was amused by the packaging. The amusement was not, however, shared by the 40,000 workers whose jobs depended on a continuous flow of financing.

In his diatribe, Ferry overestimated the indebtedness of the city – understandably, perhaps, since Haussmann had constructed a fiscal maze hard for any mere

Right: Once again Haussmann is pictured coining money from his transformation of Paris. After he was fired, he had no capital except his wife's dowry and was obliged to earn his living in a variety of jobs.

G. Lafosse

journalist to find his way through. What emerged clearly was a tendency by the prefect to underestimate costs. Such overruns were due partly to unforeseeable expenditures necessitated by unpleasant surprises – such as for example having to deal with unsuspected underground water – and partly to Haussmann's insistence on a perfect link-up of the various phases of his three programmes in order to preserve the unity of Paris.

Inevitably, the arguments for and against the baron helped generate a murky atmosphere of distrust of his administration. If the costs of Plan 3 were so much higher, as they clearly were, than those of Plan 1, why? Evidently, the money was going somewhere. No doubt into the pockets of the prefect and his rich friends! (Actually, the funds were refinancing each successive step of the reconstruction.) Only Haussmann knew how preposterous the personal accusations were. At the end of his term in office, he would have nothing with which to support himself except his wife's dowry – not even a state pension, the normal reward for a life-time of routine civil service. (In fact, he had refused such a payment out of pride.) As for those speculators who profited handsomely from Haussmann's projects, they were able to live out lives of ease and often of luxury. A visit to the mansions overlooking the Haussmann's Parc de Monceau testifies to the opulent lifestyle of the richest of the rich. A typical example is the superb Hôtel Camondo (63 Rue Monceau, 17th *Arrondissement*) entirely furnished with 18th-century masterpieces of art and craftsmanship.

In February 1869, the senate decided that the charges in the legislature against the prefect warranted a prolonged debate. A renewed treaty with the city's bank, Crédit Foncier, had to be ratified if work was to continue. Savage oratory targeted Haussmann's motives but he defended himself with honour and clarity. He had, he said, 'but one witness: Paris itself'.

'The good fortune to direct the great Paris administration through undreamed-of difficulties will remain the dominant fact of my life ... I have for the past sixteen years put aside my own interests, my personal tastes, my friend-ships – and even the joys of family life – to amass with jealous care a capital of honour. This capital will constitute the bulk of the heritage my children may look forward to.'

Haussmann always spoke softly, confident that he had in his grasp a big stick – the backing of the Emperor. One legislator opined that his speaking style was consistent with his streets – endlessly long and dull. But on this important occa-sion, he set aside his briefcase full of statistics and instead spoke from his heart. After the orators of the legislative assembly had pummelled him with scorn, ridicule and innuendo, the senate finally voted the authorisation needed to continue the third and final phase of the transformation of Paris.

But was it really a victory? Because Haussmann got what he wanted, yes. Yet in terms of their success in planting doubts about the administration's use of power, his enemies got what they really hoped for. Haussmann was never under the illusion that the attacks were basically about money, even though they were sparked by the penny-pinching legislators whose fear of investing in the transformation of Paris had led to the deplorable state of the city in 1853. He had overcome their resistance to progress then. Now, he was certain, the senate did not really want to halt the beautification of Paris – a source of pride to them as well as to the government and the public at large. Instead, the prefect knew that the volleys aimed at him were in reality intended to weaken the Emperor; in ably protecting himself, he was shielding his boss. Napoleon

III himself receded into silence, preoccupied by the complexity of his role as the key player in the deadly game of European diplomacy. Within a year, his clumsy attempts to become the power-broker of Europe would result in the disaster of the Franco–Prussian War.

But even before then, the hold of Napoleon III on power in his own country was loosening. The proof came in the legislative elections of 1869. The results of the first round of voting pointed to a clear repudiation of the government; even though the second round served to redress the situation to some degree, Paris was completely lost to the government.

Even in his private life, Haussmann made himself a high target. From 1857 to 1869, the second most important man in Paris was having an affair with a pretty, young dancer at the Opéra. Parisians found nothing especially remarkable about such a dalliance, even though Jules Ferry switched from attacking with figures to firing off quips. The Emperor himself led the way in amorous matters as he did in every walk of life. (Even the little hats his wife wore immediately became high fashion.) What titillated the scandal-mongers was that Haussmann's friend, Françoise Cellier, was a nobody. In contrast, the Emperor sported with women who were either titled or clever or both. Not only did the baron help his Françoise to get started in her theatrical career, but the increasing elegance of her successive apartments implied a knowledge of real-estate futures that was – to say the least – astonishing. (Her last address was in the Boulevard Malesherbes, one of Haussmann's most triumphant realisations, as we have seen.)

Except for the few crumbs they were able to garner from Mademoiselle Cellier's progressive lifestyle, Haussmann's enemies could hardly hope, in Paris, to reap much nourishment from the affair. To be sure, Haussmann lacked discretion, leaving his easily identifiable carriage waiting at the stage door of the Opéra (then still in the Rue Pelletier). Later, when Cellier became a (rather indifferent) singer in operettas, some of her lines about a girl's prominent protector drew titters at the wrong moments from the insiders in the audience. Nor was it normal for the *seigneur* of the palatial Hôtel de Ville to receive coveys of ballerinas there after their performance. However, such stuff was hardly likely to create a storm in a society nearly all of whose members had stories of their own to tell if they wished to do so.

However, Octavie was hurt by the gossip – most of it highly spiced. A devoted couple was coming apart. On the one hand, Haussmann in his fifties found himself physically and mentally a man half his age. Time was running on, but his body did not want to know it. And his passion for music never ebbed. (After his death, a season ticket to the Opéra was found – fully paid – among his possessions.) What could be less surprising than his affinity for a young singer who incarnated one of the joys of his own inner life?

Whereas her husband was noticeably younger than his years, the opposite was true for Octavie. Her role in Bordeaux had suited her well; as the wife of the local prefect, and hostess nurtured in the role learned from a good Bordelais family, she could be at ease among friends. But in Paris her job took on a different dimension.

The sheer scale of it dwarfed her modest temperament. Nevertheless, she performed meritoriously, if without relish. Her appearances at the Opéra must have been anguishing for her, knowing as she did of Françoise Cellier. For support, she relied more and more heavily on her faith in God. Octavie began the day in the company of her Bible, rather than that of her husband, who very likely would have been glad to talk about his starring role at last night's ball.

Was Octavie aware of the scurrilous story fabricated by the most venomous members of the opposition? Producing little more than amusing gossip, the Cellier affair was proving to be more a diversion than the kind of scandal capable of producing shock waves. Now the mud-slingers thought they could do better than that. Accordingly, they circulated an anonymous tract whose scenario has the yeasty Napoleon III yearning for a virgin. Haussmann, ever ready to oblige his boss, offers up his daughter, Fanny-Valentine. Unfortunately she becomes pregnant. To avoid a scandal, the inner circle at the Tuileries arrange for the girl to kept out of the public eye while Napoleon III's mistress, Madame Bellanger, gradually puffs up her waistline with pillows. At the proper time, she appears with 'her' child and Fanny-Valentine is able to resume her pleasure-seeking life.

Anyone familiar with Haussmann's devotion to his daughters could only sigh over such a sick story. But what about the great public with no direct knowledge of the imperious prefect?

Whether or not Octavie was aware of this trumped-up tale, she retreated to Bordeaux. Only the insistence of the Empress Eugénie, who knew a lot about husbands and gossip, brought her back to Paris.

Below: Haussmann's opponents tried, but failed to change the name of 'his' boulevard. A suggested beneficiary was a bitter critic of Haussmann, Victor Hugo. The writer, however, had his compensation; the Avenue Hugo is one of the most elegant in the city.

None of the attacks – whether on Haussmann's financial manipulations or his personal life – altered the trust that Napoleon III appeared to have in his lieutenant. After all, his prefect's imperial manner was what Napoleon III would have liked, but no longer dared, to display. He had earned a well-deserved reputation as an adroit and ruthless politician. As such, he read correctly the message the electorate was sending him: that his authoritarian ways were alienating much of the population. He veered to the left, yielding more liberty of expression to the people and increased power to the legislature.

While the rumblings from the people were being heard by his boss, Haussmann appeared to be tone deaf – a strange ailment in a person who prided himself on his political awareness. Even as the style of the head of government became more conciliatory, the baron-prefect-senator continued to harangue legislators and ministers. Haussmann had his great work to complete and nothing would distract him from finishing it in his usual uncompromising fashion. As long as he continued to have the support of the Emperor, no one could stand in his way. With it, he was able to soldier on throughout the year 1869.

By the beginning of that year, most of the demolition and rebuilding of the centre of Paris had been achieved. For the first time in sixteen years there was a period of relative calm. Parisians could enjoy their elegant new city, with its promenades, open vistas, fountains and green spaces. Meanwhile, the great work of Haussmannisation (as it came to be called) continued as frenetically as ever, but now in the western part of the city, where the land was largely unoccupied and the need for demolition minimal. The handsome *mairie* of Passy (16th *Arrondissement*) is notable as the last important public building erected under Haussmann's regime.

Little did Haussmann suspect that the approval of funding for the last phase of his work probably resulted from a deal Napoleon III finally struck with the opposition. The senators wanted the work to go on – but without Haussmann. Under pressure, the Emperor let it be understood that, in return for the needed ratification loans, he was prepared to disavow his support of his prefect.

On 2 January 1870 Napoleon III named Emile Ollivier, the leader of the opposition, to head the government. Haussmann had known Ollivier abrasively for twenty years, first as a radical leader in the *Département* of the Var. There the young prefect Haussmann had been forced to keep him under constant surveillance as a troublemaker and a threat to the government. Later he proved also to be a slippery politician and - unlike Haussmann - an orator with a golden tongue. The hostility of the two men from opposite ends of the political spectrum was such that Haussmann once decided that he would resign if the other ever came to power. However, when that time arrived, he was not given the chance to step down in a way that he found acceptable. In demanding Haussmann's resignation, Ollivier stipulated that it could not be effective until he had formed his new government and found a replacement for the Prefect. This drew from the baron a statement of his most profound political conviction: he would never consent, even temporarily, to become a part of a new mongrel 'Parliamentary Empire' which he characterised as 'the beginning of the end' for France. (This was prophetic; before the year was out, France and Prussia were locked in a war that ended disastrously for France, gave birth to the horrors of the Paris Commune and brought into being the Third Republic.)

On 6 January the new cabinet was in place. The stand-off was broken by a letter from the Emperor, signed that day. Haussmann was fired. That Napoleon III felt no joy at having to choose practicality over preference is confirmed by the fact that the two men met for two hours the same afternoon. What was said remains unknown.

The next day, Haussmann went before the municipal council to say farewell. For seventeen years he had cajoled and goaded the council into approving measure after measure necessary for the transformation of Paris. Through it all, the members came to appreciate his intelligence and unflagging energy. That day the ex-prefect was calm but understandably bitter. 'One must have courage and devotion', he said, 'to enter public service in France, there to consecrate energy and abilities that in another profession would win him independence and a fortune instead of antagonism and misunderstanding ...'

That appearance was only a warm-up for his final grand performance. As was to be expected, the new Minister of the Interior, M. Chavandier de Valdrôme, convoked formally all the high officials of the government to a meeting on 10 January. Among the invitations issued was one addressed, simply, to '*le préfet de la Seine*'. Since his successor had not yet arrived in Paris, Haussmann decided, with relish, to accept. He donned his most splendid uniform and ordered out his gilded carriages with their colourfully dressed coachmen and footmen. To top this off, he arrived at the reception escorted by the even more majestic Garde de Paris. Such an arrival could hardly pass unnoticed!

The minister and his officers, also in full dress, received him immediately. Haussmann entered, flanked by his retinue, and announced that he was there to declare 'his full support of the Emperor'.

Not a word about the new minister. In fact, this official was the son of one of Haussmann's first powerful backers, Casimir Perier. The son, Auguste, had cast his vote against the prefect, but now he said, hands outstretched, how much he regretted the 'realities of politics'.

Haussmann straightened to his full, imposing height and bowed slightly.

'Monsieur le ministre, he replied. 'I am especially flattered by your appreciation of my career and of my work in Paris because your words are so unexpected.'

Then he went on: 'I entered the administrative service of France under the ministry of the illustrious Casimir Perier in 1831. Your venerated father was at that time one of my principal sponsors. I couldn't be more happy that his son, 38 years after, and now minister in his turn, sees fit to recognise that I have not failed to live up to his father's expectations.'

He awaited no reply. A flick of the whip from his coachman and he left behind him the men of intrigue.

'Haussmann the Magnificent!' Perhaps the British had it right.

EPILOGUE

When Haussmann returned to the Hôtel de Ville, Octavie was busy packing to go back to her beloved Bordeaux. Her husband left Paris with his head held high, but his destination was not Bordeaux; he took off for a point in France about as far from Paris as it is possible to go. He needed to be alone – to come to terms, if possible, with what had happened to him.

As a well-paid civil servant, the prefect had been able to purchase a small villa on a hillside between Nice and Villefranche-sur-Mer on the Mediterranean coast. There he found the peace he required. The villa had been converted from premises housing an olive-oil press. His loyal friend and associate, Alphand, designed the landscaping, punctuating the silvery green of olive leaves with the brilliance of a grove of orange trees. This led to a neighbouring house occupied by another long-time friend, a M. Frémy, an interior-department general-secretary and supporter of the prefect for more than twenty years.

A lovely place to rest and recuperate, but Haussmann's limited ability to endure inactivity quickly wore thin. Within six months he was back in Paris, attending the races at the elegant Longchamp track, a Haussmann creation which he rated high among his achievements. Across the field from the stadium, surrounded in June by greenery, stands a small and charming château that Napoleon III had presented to him and Octavie as a refuge from the turmoil of their life at the Hôtel de Ville.

Probably Haussmann was not surprised that his old boss was attending the famous Grand Prix races that day. Napoleon III spotted his former lieutenant in the stands and sent for him, warmly shaking his hand and proposing that they meet next day for lunch and a 'quiet chat' at the Palace of St-Cloud. In his memoirs, which he now had time to work on, the baron remembered that meeting as an extraordinary event. According to the third volume, the Emperor told Haussmann of his discontent with the new government, even to the point of branding his ministers as 'incompetent'. He then confided that he was considering a re-organisation that would bring Georges-Eugène back into an even greater position of power than before.

Perhaps the conversation was not as explicit as Haussmann recalled, but events soon lent support to his version of the meeting. A month later Napoleon III left Paris to take command of the French forces facing Prussia's awesome war machine. Finally, the Empress Eugénie had her hands on the levers of power. Confirming her husband's opinion that the government was weak and confused, she and Emile Ollivier, Haussmann's old foe, decided to form a new cabinet. The first and only person the Empress's advisers approached to become a key player was none other than the baron. (Ollivier belatedly recognised in Haussmann 'the strength and lucidity' needed at such a desperate hour.) The former prefect accepted – with one proviso: that the Emperor return to Paris to take charge of a situation that was fast running out of control. In no mood to give up her position of power, Eugénie refused.

The stand-off determined the course of the rest of Georges-Eugène's life – and perhaps the future of France itself. Still a senator, he only had time to make a stirring speech urging the local authorities and the French population to fight with anything at their disposal: shovels to dig ditches across roads to slow the advancing Germans, axes to fell trees, hunting rifles, overturned carts. Any action whatsoever, other than the shameful retreat that was now under way. But no one in the government seemed to have the stomach for such stern measures. Word soon spread of the fall of the key city of Sedan and then of Napoleon's capture by the Prussians at Châlons-sur-Marne. The day after Haussmann's inspired speech, the mob took over the defence of Paris. Wasn't that, in a sense, what Haussmann had been urging – the defence of the nation by its citizens? After all, the government had sadly failed the people and the people were rising up. But resistance to a foreign invader was one thing; what the Commune stood for was another: civil war, class against class, carried out on a wave of terror. On 4 September 1870, the government abdicated and the Third Republic was born out of the ashes of the Second Empire. The Avenue 4 Septembre – christened that very day – is one of those connecting the working-class eastern part of the city with the Place de

Left: Consigned to storage for almost 100 years after the prefect's death, this powerful statue of the Baron Haussmann today overlooks the boulevard that carries his name. It was dedicated on 13 September 1989 by the then-mayor of Paris, Jacques Chirac, in the presence of Madame Gérard Haussmann and others.

l'Opéra, the most opulent public building created during the Haussmann transformations, as well as the Boulevard des Capucines, the promenade of the rich and famous under King Louis XIV.

The symbol in Paris of all of the sins of the Empire, the Baron would have been mad to remain in a city gone mad. Victor Hugo, returning from exile in the Channel Island of Guernsey even announced that soon the Boulevard Haussmann would be renamed as – no surprise – the Boulevard Victor Hugo. He never had that satisfaction; the turmoil was such, amidst burning buildings, shootings, starvation and terror, that no one got around to acting on the suggestion, though one of the important avenues radiating from the Arc de Triomphe – as well as the Place Victor Hugo – bears his name.

There was no way even a Haussmann could fight the monster of revenge that was the Paris Commune. Stifling his pride – he had never before run away from a mob – he decided to decamp for Bordeaux.

Surely beyond his imagination was the greeting that awaited him in his adopted city, home of his wife's family, and the birthplace of his children. The radicals had succeeded in making their shrill voice heard throughout the land. Outside his former prefecture a mob shouting 'Arrest Haussmann' was in full cry. The incumbent prefect, alarmed, telegraphed Paris: 'Should I arrest him?' Fortunately, he got no reply.

Despite the furore, Haussmann could reason that the Communists of Paris would find joy in attacking the lackey, as Haussmann was often called, of Napoleon III. A far more severe blow turned out to be his frosty reception by the families among whom he had formerly been *chez lui*. In a city where he had been its most powerful figure, the doors of the bourgeois homes, where he had so often dined, wined and discussed the affairs of the day, were closed. Seventeen years earlier he had left the city with a fabulous career before him. Now he was returning as worse than a stranger – a disgraced bureaucrat whose past achievements went unrecognised, whose present image was that of a pariah and whose dubious future was darkened further by urgent money problems.

The Emperor's words of regret at the time of Haussmann's dismissal had been accompanied by a generous offer of a lump-sum severance payment. Out of pride, the prefect had refused to accept it, leaving him with only a civil service retirement pay of 6,000 francs a month. However, his refusal probably made no difference; events were unravelling with such speed that the money probably would not have reached him in any case.

Why was he shunned by the local bourgeoisie after having transformed the centre of Paris into a bourgeois enclave modelled largely on Bordeaux? In fact, his former friends never had been very attached to the Second Empire. The zeal of Haussmann himself had been largely responsible for support of the local voters for Napoleon III. The hearts of the conservative burghers of the region had always been with the fallen monarchy. Now, in another period of political turmoil, their nostalgia took over.

Octavie was of little comfort. Saintly as she was, she retreated more and more within herself. A photograph taken a year earlier shows her dressed in black, wearing a little lace cap and sitting stiffly upright on the very edge of a hard chair. She is looking at the camera with vague disapproval. In their hostile environment, she was afraid for her husband's safety. Little persuasion was needed on her part to convince Haussmann that he needed a rest and should seek it somewhere else. Once again, his villa on the road to Villefranche beckoned.

In contrast to Octavie, Haussmann at 71 was still young in body and spirit. In a re-issue of his book, now entitled *Haussmann: La Gloire du Deuxième Empire* (Editions Perrin, Paris, 1988), the historian Jean des Cars says that he has unearthed evidence that Octavie's devotion went far beyond a wife's traditional duty. It seems that her sense of charity even reached out to Françoise Cellier when the dancer fled the Commune. Not only did Octavie find her a place to stay (at a discreet distance from Bordeaux); when Haussmann took off for Villefranche, his friend Mademoiselle Cellier was beside him in the coach.

Soon the baron had evidence that the provisional government in Paris was tracking his movements. His villa was broken into and his papers ransacked. In addition, the local prefect was asked to report on Haussmann's health. 'Fine,' was his response. 'He lunched here today.'

From across the French–Italian border only a few kilometres away, Rome beckoned. In Italy, he was well known, celebrated for his transformation of Paris. Shuttling from city to city, he tried to divert his mind from the after-taste of his downfall, made doubly painful by the cold shoulder that had greeted his return to Bordeaux. A Florentine banker bolstered his morale with a proposition: to direct the rejuvenation of Rome. In the end, the baron refused, perhaps because his reverence for the glories of Imperial Rome made him shrink from the demolition that would have been necessary. He simply made some suggestions on a map, which has since disappeared.

Meanwhile, civil war tore Haussmann's Paris apart. At the start of the Commune, raw excavations of interrupted projects scarred the city. Then came the bombardments as the French government in Versailles joined forces with the Prussians to defeat the Commune. Finally, on the night of 24 May 1871, the Communards torched the Hôtel de Ville. 'We have just lighted up the château Haussmann,' they cried. The handsome building burned for eight days, destroying innumerable precious files and documents. What the visitor sees today is its replacement, larger and more lavishly decorated, but in general respecting the configuration of the original. Flames danced and flickered throughout the city, Napoleon III's palace of the Tuileries fuelling the biggest bonfire of all.

More adept at writing about balance sheets and administration than communicating his inner feelings, Haussmann leaves us to imagine his reaction to the destruction on all sides. In fact – given the dimensions of the disaster – France and Paris recovered with astonishing speed. The Third Republic continued the ex-prefect's work as though he were now seated in the new Hôtel de Ville. His team and his plans were still intact. Chief engineer Belgrand finished the great reservoir at the Parc du Montsouris in tandem with the faithful Alphand who completed work on the park itself. Now that Haussmann was destroyed politically, the uproar

Right: This photograph showing Haussmann near the time of his death is actually based on an earlier, more youthful photograph, retouched for the occasion.

about financing ceased. Even as the nation was paying off with astonishing ease the enormous indemnities imposed by the treaty of peace, the city went on to complete the third part of the ex-prefect's plan

In 1875 the Opéra – afterwards to be called 'le Palais Garnier' by Parisians, was completed. The year 1877 saw the opening of the Avenue de l'Opéra, but traffic did not start flowing along the Avenue de la République until 1889. Finally, in 1927 – fifty-seven years after its namesake was hounded from office by the politicians of the day! – the final extension of the Boulevard Haussmann (between the Rue Taitbout and the Rue Drouot) was opened.

Less important streets continued to be created or widened – all of them Haussmannian, the buildings of dressed stone, with balconies of intricate iron-work and boasting imposing entrances, sufficiently tall and wide to receive carriages and loftily perched coachmen, These grandiose *portes cochères* continued to feature long after the automobile had defeated the horse and carriage, their height reduced but their appearance little changed by the installation of a window at the level of the first floor. During the years leading up to the First World War, the façades became increasingly ornate, but the basic Haussmannian character continued to prevail. The Art Nouveau of Guimard was simply a detour en route to the 1920s when such architects as Mallet-Stevens and Le Corbusier called a halt, celebrating efficiency and simplicity over decoration. (Examples of the work

Below: The Evangelical Lutheran Church of the Redemption, 16 Rue Chauchat, Haussmann's church and scene of his funeral. The curious façade is due to the construction of the church within a former warehouse for taxable goods entering Paris, a practice the baron ended.

of both men can be seen, conveniently close to each other, in the Rue Docteur Blanche, 16th *Arrondissement*.)

Haussmann hoped to produce a source of revenue from the vineyards attached to the Château Cesta, which Octavie had inherited in 1862. It was – and is – a pleasant place, only 30 kilometres south of Bordeaux. The château even shows the handiwork of the celebrated architect Baltard who redesigned the façade. At the same time, Haussmann enlarged the vineyards on the property and succeeded in producing a good-quality wine. But the vines fell victim to a fungal disease and his income fell far short of his needs in a time of rapidly rising prices. Haussmann found himself a poor man, forced to live on borrowed funds – an intolerable situation for a man of pride.

Finding a job was no longer a matter of choice. Happily, he had strong links with the Pereire brothers, whose banking house had financed the development of a vast area around the Parc Monceau. And the links were personal as well as financial. Twenty-one years earlier, Haussmann's elder daughter, Marie-Henriette, then twenty years old, had announced her decision to marry a young employee in her father's prefecture. Haussmann was having none of it. The unfortunate young man found himself propelled to an insignificant post in rural France. Three weeks later, Marie-Henriette went to the altar. At her side was young Camille Dollfus, son of a partner in the Pereire banking empire. Who can say that Marie-Henriette was any more or less happy as Madame Dollfus than if romance had triumphed? In any case, two decades later she was still Madame Dollfus and the mother of four children adored by their grandfather.

One of the Pereire enterprises was the bank Crédit Immobilier, founded in 1852, just before Haussmann's arrival in Paris as Prefect of the Seine. Formed to help industries finance their expansion, the bank's affairs suffered from the war. Haussmann turned out to be the perfect choice to re-animate the enterprise. That job brought with it his last chance to take control of a major urban project. A year earlier, a large part of Constantinople – today Istanbul – had been devastated by fire. Now the city faced a huge problem of rebuilding. Haussmann spent three months there, drawing up plans and calculating the probable cost of reconstruction. It was time and effort wasted; when the time came to get down to work, the city treasury was empty – a discovery that prompted the bank to pull out.

In January 1873, soon after the baron's return, Paris received word of the death of Napoleon III at Chislehurst in England, almost exactly twenty years after Haussmann took office as Prefect of the Seine. Despite his detestation of the government, he turned up at the Elysée Palace in his prefect's uniform to pay his respects to the man he had served so well. Every year for the rest of his life, he would attend memorial services marking the death of Napoleon III.

As his usefulness to Crédit Immobilier faded, he added another post in 1884 – that of president of the administration of an important group of warehouses and retail stores with which he remained connected for the remainder of his life. During his period in the commercial world, Haussmann once again demonstrated his questing mind as well as his ability to get in step with the future. He not only applied for a patent to generate electricity by a new method, but, even more ahead of his time, he also sought a patent for a solar-powered motor – more than a century before Mitsubishi paraded on world-wide television its first car propelled by the rays of the sun.

Any portrayal of the Baron Haussmann as a sad and lonely old man, friendless and nursing his grudges, hardly seems to be supported by the facts. He had friends (more than 200 people would later accompany his casket on its journey to the cemetery), but growing old is especially disagreeable to a man of such vitality. People forgot him. Others died. He never had quite enough money (even after selling his villa in Villefranche-sur-Mer), but he was able to hold on to Cesta, which gave him a change from the bustle of Paris and a place to receive his children and grandchildren. The baron was wounded by the ingratitude and injustice he had experienced, but defeated, never.

He even wrote and published poems celebrating his romantic conquests in St-Girons. Clearly, tracking down arms smugglers in the Pyrenees had not been his only sport during his short period there as sub-prefect. Octavie's reaction to these purple verses remains unknown – if indeed she ever read them. In another poem, he refers to Alfred de Musset, one of France's greatest poets, saying that he, Haussmann, was a superior poet when they were classmates. He does get around to granting that Musset produced some good stuff later on, if 'sometimes a bit overly sentimental'. *Haussmann uber alles.*

Below: The mausoleum of the Haussmann family where the baron is buried. The neighbouring tomb to its right is that of Alfred de Musset, Haussmann's boyhood classmate and, later inspiration when he himself began, in his retirement, to write poetry.

At the age of 68, he entered elective politics for the first time, in a campaign to become the representative to the national legislature from the island of Corsica, where Napoleon I was born. This passage in his career can only be described as bizarre. The son of Napoleon III, the Prince Imperial, was still alive at the time. He and his mother, the former Empress, wanted his cousin, Jerome Napoleon, defeated in the legislative elections. Not only were there questions about Jerome's character (he was widely known as Plon-Plon), but he seems to have been guilty of flirting with the Republicans. Once again – this time from her exile in England, Eugénie remembered the merits of Haussmann – his drive and his loyalty.

Right: This ivory crucifix, a gift of Haussmann to his Church of the Redemption, looked down on the modest gathering attending his funeral. Not a single city or national official showed up to honour the creator of a reborn Paris.

What followed is stupefying. Haussmann, a non-resident of Corsica – the ancestral home of the Bonaparte family – entered the lists against a descendant of Napoleon I, the man whose grandeur won Haussmann's life-long admiration for the imperial model. But that's not all. A Protestant, the baron campaigned in a solidly Catholic electorate with the blessing of the Catholic hierarchy!

He not only won the election; he received twice as many votes as Plon-Plon.

What is not astonishing is the nature of Haussmann's most notable contribution to the well-being of Corsica. The island is a mosaic of mountains, snow-capped in winter, valleys and a tattered shore-line. Poor roads, barely passable in bad weather, periodically cut off not only remote villages clinging to dizzying mountainsides, but even the few towns on the island. The Haussmann who could not bear the isolation of the *quartiers* within post-medieval Paris, found the lack of interconnectness between the islanders unacceptable. He persuaded the Paris legislature that a railway must be built to link the capital Ajaccio with Bastia to the north. The result was an engineering feat that still wins admiration – a railway line, threading over canyons and mountainside, of such scenic splendour that visitors ride it not in order to 'get somewhere', as Haussmann had envisaged, but out of sheer pleasure.

True always to his passion for speeding the transport of goods and people, he also fought, though unsuccessfully, for the construction of a canal across France that would link the Rhine river to the French ports on the Atlantic.

This was a time when the socialist government was seeking every means available to scrub the Second Empire from the history of 19th-century France. Street

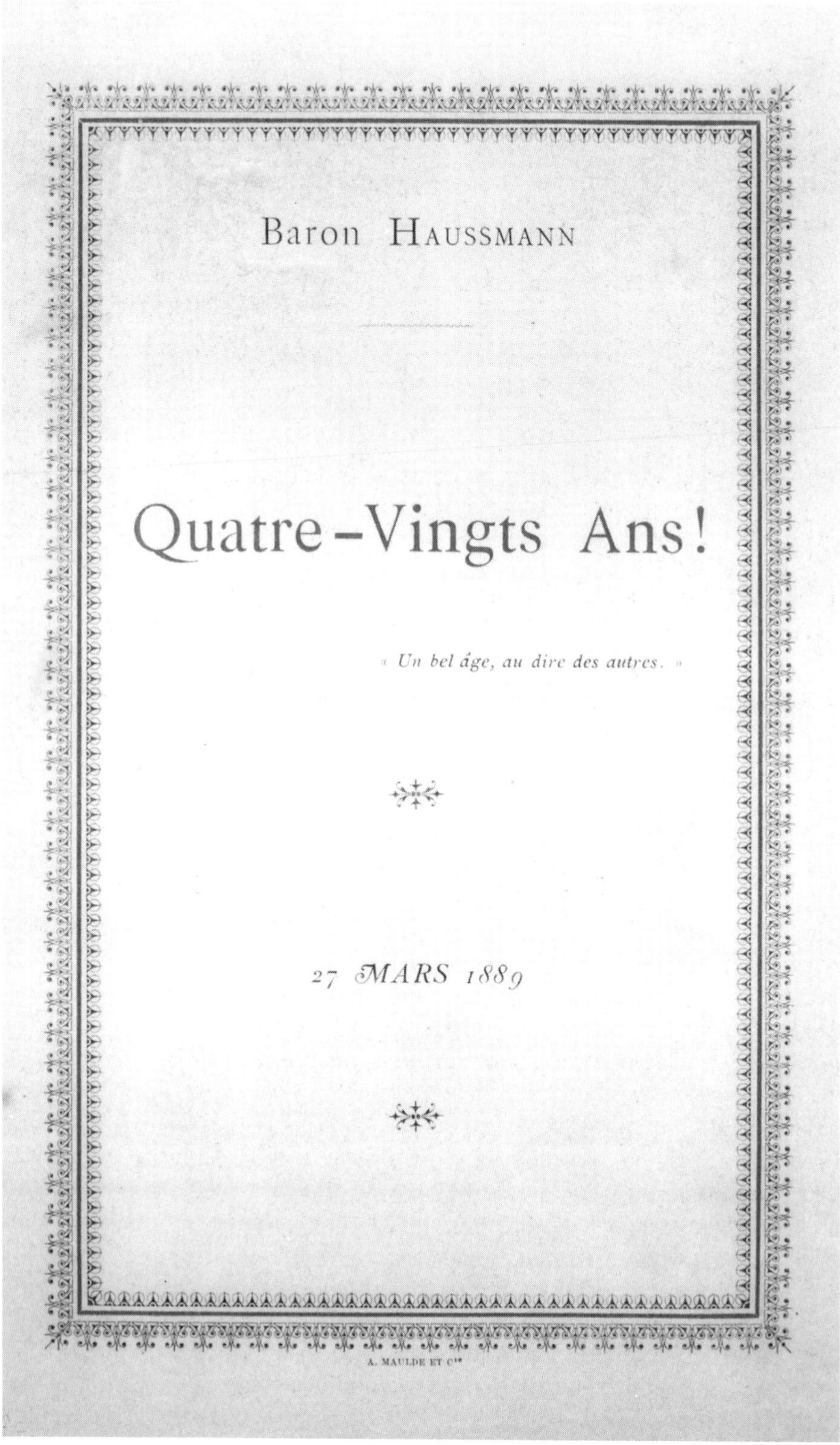

Baron HAUSSMANN

Quatre-Vingts Ans!

« Un bel âge, au dire des autres. »

27 MARS 1889

A. MAULDE ET Cie

Left and right: *Baron Haussmann loved, and often wrote, poetry, especially as he grew older. The above was printed to present to friends who joined him in the celebration of his 80th birthday. (Document courtesy Madame Gérard Haussmann.)*

QUATRE-VINGTS ANS !

« Un bel âge, au dire des autres. »

C'est fête, et c'est aussi chose bien sérieuse,
La quatrième fois qu'on accomplit vingt ans !
Or, de mon nouveau cycle, aujourd'hui, le printemps
Vient de naître bien froid et d'humeur soucieuse ;
Car il tombe en plein krach. Cependant, malgré tout,
Je suis ragaillardi, vrai ! par votre présence,
Et ce dernier début de ma longue existence
Me prend jeune toujours de cœur, d'esprit, de goût.

N'était quelque raideur de mes reins, de mes jambes,
Je me croirais encore en mil huit cent vingt-neuf,
Quand j'entrai dans le monde, alerte, battant neuf,
Bon pied, bon œil. rendant des points aux plus ingambes :
Féru du Beau, du Grand ; prompt à l'illusion
Peut-être bien ; menant l'Art et la Poésie
De pair avec l'Étude, avec la jalousie
D'atteindre un noble but, avec la passion
De servir mon pays, de suivre une carrière
Où je pusse acquérir l'Honneur, sinon l'Argent.
Je narguais le Veau d'or, et fus trop négligent
De ce Dieu de nos jours, durant ma course entière !..

Mais, pour m'en corriger, il se fait un peu tard.
Je suis payé. du reste, avec l'autre monnaie,
Bien assez largement pour que jamais je n'aie
A regretter mon choix. La Poésie et l'Art
Ont charmé les tourments, les dégoûts, que la vie
Ne m'a pas épargnés. Hors de mes fonctions,
J'ai su grouper, d'ailleurs, nombre d'affections
Pour m'en faire un Trésor, le plus digne d'envie.

En ce jour, où l'usage est de former des vœux,
Je demande à garder, sans krach, cette fortune,
Jusqu'au moment d'aller, suivant la loi commune,
Me reposer, enfin, où dorment les aïeux.

EIGHTY YEARS

A fine age – they say

A celebration, but also a very serious matter,
Rounding out twenty years for the fourth time!
Now, to usher in a new cycle, springtime
Has just been born, cold and spiteful,
Spitting down rain in cascades, No matter,
I am uplifted, truly, by your presence,
And this last debut of my long existence
Finds me still young at heart, in spirit and in zest.

A certain stiffness of back and legs aside,
I could believe myself still twenty,
Entering the adult world, alert, spanking new,
Strong of foot, of eye, ceding a head start to the more nimble,
In love with the beautiful, the august, prey of illusions,
Perhaps good, melding art and poetry
And study, with a determination
To achieve a noble goal and with a passion
To serve my country, to pursue a career
Where I could acquire honor, if not money
I've spurned the golden calf, and have been too negligent
Of this god of our times throughout my life !.

However it is a little late to correct this fault,
Besides, I have been paid in another coin,
Indeed so generously that I have never
Regretted my choice, Poetry and Art
Have soothed the torments, the disgust, that life
Hasn't spared me. And outside of my work,
I've been able to find a circle of kindred souls
To constitute a treasury more worthy of envy.

This day, when the custom is to state a wish,
I ask to cherish this fortune intact, seamless,
Until the moment to go, in accordance with common law,
To rest, finally, where our ancestors sleep.

Left: A translation of the poem presented to friends on his 80th birthday (see previous spread).

names were being changed. Even the name of Napoleon III was relegated to near-extinction by being attached to a tiny square in a corner of the 10th *Arrondissement*. (In the otherwise exhaustive *'Dictionnaire des noms des Rues de Paris'* the square is not even mentioned.)

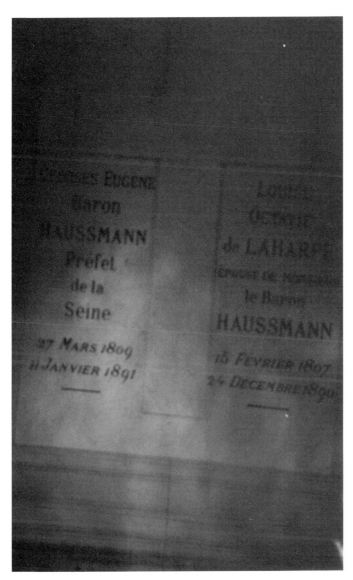

None the less, the Boulevard Haussmann remains one of the principal arteries of Paris. The baron may have escaped the humiliation of having his name removed because he remained a member of the Chamber of Deputies (formerly the Legislative Assembly); presumably even the most bitter enemies of the Second Empire shrank from administering such a blow to a fellow legislator sitting in their midst.

Once again Haussmann demonstrated his knack for finding noble words worthy of the occasion: 'Inscriptions can be changed. But as long as Paris lives, my name will be engraved on every stone.'

He decided not to run in the elections of 1881. His sponsor, the prince Imperial, son of Napoleon III and Eugénie, had died in Africa under a hail of Zulu assegais. Haussmann had performed the job the prince had assigned to him by removing Plon-Plon from public life. He had no wish to continue to be embroiled in family politics, even if that had been possible, now that he was deprived of the backing of the late son of Napoleon III.

For ten years, the rebuilding of the Hôtel de Ville had been under way, while the blackened ruins of the Tuileries Palace remained untouched.

Above: A glimpse of inscriptions inside Haussmann's tomb. Important to note: he died just fifteen days after his wife Octavie.

For Haussmann both buildings spoke of past glory – of France, of himself, of the Second Empire. Not only had the Tuileries been the home of Napoleon III, but also that of his uncle, Napoleon I, Haussmann's idol. In 1879, he rose from his seat in the Chamber of Deputies to make an impassioned plea for the reconstruction of the palace. He spoke with authority when he pointed out that much of the building was salvageable, even suggesting that damaged stones could be replaced by making impressions of the originals. The restored building would, he asserted, form a splendid home for a museum of modern art. For once, 'Haussmann the ripper' was proposing restoration rather than demolition. However, neither the republican Deputies nor the city council were disposed to preserve a monument to imperial France. In 1882, they ordered the destruction of the palace.

Following the basic lines of the original, the spectacular Hôtel de Ville that visitors flock to see today was inaugurated on 14 July, the anniversary of the French Revolution. The great and less-so were invited to the ceremony, but one person was notably omitted from the guest list – he who from the south-west wing of the building had presided over the beautification of the surrounding area, then over the reconstruction of the entire city and finally over the integration of the suburbs that doubled the size of Paris. His glorious receptions for the powerful, the royalty and the glamorous of the world had made the Hôtel de Ville the sparkling centre of Europe. Now the former host found himself uninvited to the reception where he should have been the most honoured of guests.

Such peevishness was a part of the campaign to write Haussmann out of the history of Paris. Terribly hurt, he faced the spectre of becoming forgotten. To create for the record a complete account and justification of his life's work, he set about writing his memoirs which finally filled three massive volumes. (He had planned a fourth, but death intervened.) They are boastful, often dull, and without any suggestion that he himself might have nourished the level of hostility he generated among so many people. In heaping praise on himself, he illustrates, rather than recognises, his major short-coming: that of hubris. None the less, the facts and documents he marshalled speak not only of his brilliance as an administrator but also of his devotion to detail.

By the time the three volumes were finished, their author was 80 years old, but the good health with which he had been blessed throughout his adult years remained with him. 'I may be aged,' he declared, 'but I am not yet an old man.' In a poem, he referred to himself as 'an old lion'.

From his modest three-roomed Paris apartment at 12 Rue Boissy d'Anglas (8th *Arrondissement*), the old lion would emerge to stroll the streets of 'his' city and so became aware of a fact that no one had bothered to tell him: that the continued transformation of Paris was following, unmodified, his Plan 3. Not only that, but he was often recognised by passers-by. Exchanging nods from time to time reassured him of his continued existence, despite the best efforts of officialdom to forget it. He divided his time between Paris and Cesta where he was saluted as the 'Grand Baron' during his rides around the neighbourhood.

Such small pleasures couldn't shield him from the penalties that go with living a long life. Others – less fortunate? – disappeared one by one. Most painful to Georges-Eugène were the deaths of those close to him: his sister, Caroline, in 1885; a grandson, then the boy's mother, Marie-Henriette, who died in 1890 at the age of 51.

On Christmas Eve of 1891, it became the turn of Octavie to go. Nevertheless, on 9 January 1892, the Baron Haussmann showed up at Baltard's Church of St-Augustin (8th *Arrondissement*) for the memorial service to Napoleon III, his record intact of never having missed one of these annual ceremonies. Next day he was again in full uniform, his chest heavy with medals, as he appeared at the funeral of a member of the Russian Imperial family, the Grand Duke Nicolas of

Leuchtenberg. Defying the frigid weather, the baron decided to follow the funeral cortege to the Russian Orthodox Church in the Rue Daru, in the 17th *Arrondissement*.

The decision proved unwise. The following evening he received a group of friends for dinner in his apartment. After the meal, they stayed to chat before the fire. In mid-sentence Georges-Eugène was convulsed by pain in his chest. His guests summoned a doctor who arrived an hour later. By that time, the baron had apparently recovered and was again exchanging views with his friends. The physician was not fooled. He detected a ruptured blood vessel and ordered his patient to bed. Haussmann obeyed reluctantly, insisting on undressing himself.

He died 30 minutes later. Faithful at last to the ever faithful Octavie, he joined her only eighteen days after her death.

Haussmann's funeral did no honour to the city of Paris nor the national government. The services were held in the tiny Lutheran Church of the Redemption in the motley Rue Chauchat. It is a bare oak-panelled church with only 24 rows of wooden pews. Behind the altar stands a large crucifix in ivory – a gift from Georges-Eugène Haussmann. Not a single official of the state or the city of Paris was present, only a representative of the Légion d'honneur, sent in accordance with the rules of the Legion.

One augury that Haussmann's memory would not be so readily effaced came when the cortege gathered at his home to accompany the hearse to the church and then on to the cemetery of Père Lachaise. Behind the three masters of ceremonies, displaying on black pillows the wealth of medals awarded to the baron, an estimated 300 people gathered to follow the casket. One can safely guess that they included past associates (Alphand, for one, was there), family, friends – among them those who had gathered from time to time for intimate dinners in the Rue Boissy d'Anglas – and Parisians grateful for the elegant new Paris Haussmann bequeathed to them.

The black hearse, pulled by a plodding black horse, followed a very Haussmannian route – from the magnificent Place de la Concorde, along the Rue de Rivoli to the Place Vendôme, then past the now completed Opéra and along the grand Boulevards Capucine and Italiens to the Rue Pelletier, site of the old Opera House where Haussmann had spent so many pleasurable hours, certain of them naughty, and on to the cemetery.

Nothing distinguishes Haussmann's tomb from the little row of houses of the dead typical of the time except an inscription carved in the stone above the door: 'La Famille Haussmann'. No special attention is called to the baron himself or to his work. Yet on one side the genius of his classmate, Alfred de Musset, is proclaimed (in a poem de Musset wrote that he wanted to be buried under a willow tree. And so he is). On the other side is the vault of another friend, the writer Arsène de Houssaye, whose genius is also proclaimed in stone. Not so, Haussmann's.

The absence of official pomp or glorification that day might have consigned Haussmann to the dustbin of history, as his enemies hoped. Time, however, would prove bricks and mortar more durable than spite. Hadn't Haussmann said it himself fourteen years earlier? 'As long as Paris lives, my name will be inscribed on every stone.'

In 1991 the city of Paris took over the maintenance of his mausoleum. The same year, nearly 100 years after his death, his statue, mysteriously hidden away in storage, was finally brought to light and erected – perhaps, more accurately, resurrected – at the intersection of the Boulevard Haussmann and the Avenue de Messine. Appropriately, the statue stands on a base of *pierre de taille*, the dressed stone excavated from the bowels of Paris for the construction of buildings throughout the city; they are today identified as Haussmannian.

FOCAL POINTS
BY ARRONDISSEMENT

Here the illustrations in this book are grouped by *arrondissement* in order to help a visitor to any single site to move on to others in the same *arrondissement* with the use of a standard guide-book organised by *arrondissement*.

BIBLIOGRAPHY – AND READERS' GUIDE

General Sources in English

Christiansen, Rupert, *Tales of the New Babylon, Paris in the mid-19th Century*, Mandarin, London, 1996. Focusing on the Commune that took over Paris at the end of the Franco-Prussian War.

Jordan, David P, *Transforming Paris, The Life and Labors of Baron Haussmann*. The Free Press, New York, 1995. A scholarly but highly judgemental biography.

McMillan, James F, *Napoleon III*, Macmillan, New York, 1993. A compact biography of Haussmann's boss.

Saalman, Howard, *Haussmann: Paris Transformed*. George Brazillier, New York, 1971. Mostly in the context of urban planning.

General Sources in French

Des Cars, Jean, *Haussmann, La Gloire du Second République*, Librairie Académique, Perrin, Paris, 1988. The most readable and complete biography of Haussmann still in print in 1999.

Frerejean, Allain, *Napoleon IV, un Destin Brisé*, Editions Albin Michel, Paris, 1997. The tragic history of the emperor's son.

Gimard, Louis, *Napoleon III*, Fayard, Paris, 1986. A classic.

Haussmann, Georges-Eugène, *Mémoires* (Three volumes), Editions Guy Durier, Neuilly-sur-Seine, 1979. Detailed and self-justifying, a work to test the patience of most readers.

Lemeyre, Gérard, *Haussmann, Préfet de Paris*, Flammarion, Paris, 1958. An exhaustive, but not exhausting, biography, alas out of print.

Morère, Philippe, *Haussmann, Sous-Préfet Saint-Girons*, (Part I of the volume 'Moi, Baron Haussman, Sous-Préfet de Saint-Girons),

Editions Boulbi, Pamiers, 1991. A close-up of Haussmann's 20 months in the department of Ariège.

Morizet, André, *Du Vieux Paris au Paris Moderne*, Hachette, Paris, 1932, Defines Haussmann's role in the context of 19th-century Paris.

Le Pavillon d'Arsenal, Haussmann-Paris, Picard, Paris, 1991. A collection of copiously illustrated articles by Jean des Cars, Pierre Pinon and others published in connection with the 100th anniversary of Haussmann's death.

Thézv. Marie de, *Marville/Paris*. Editions Hazan, Paris, 1994. More than 600 photographs by Marville plus text. Unfortunately, the quality of reproduction fails to do full justice to Marville's work.

Touttain, Pierre André. *Haussmann*. Grund, Paris, 1971. Undoubtedly the most handsome book on the subject. Colour plates.

More specialised sources (in French)

Gaillard, Marc, *Les Fontaines de Paris*, Martell Editions, Amiens, undated.

Hillaret, Jacques, *Dictionnaire Historique des Rues de Paris* (in two volumes), Editions de Minuit, Paris, 1981. The fruit of a stupendous research into the history of every street of Paris.

Salette, Patrick, *A la Découverte des Souterrains de Paris, Sides*, 92160 Anthony, 1992. Everything a layman needs to know about the water supply and disposal system created by Haussmann. Striking photographs.

Stéphane, Bernard, *Le Dictionnaire des Noms des Rues,* Editions Mengès, 1978, Paris. How each street of Paris got its name.

INDEX